HOW TO IMPACT
and
INFLUENCE
OTHERS

James Merritt

HARVEST HOUSE PUBLISHERS

EUGENE, OREGON

Unless otherwise indicated, all Scripture quotations are from the Holy Bible, New International Version®, NIV®. Copyright © 1973, 1978, 1984 by Biblica, Inc.™ Used by permission of Zondervan. All rights reserved worldwide.

Verses marked ESV are from The Holy Bible, English Standard Version, copyright © 2001 by Crossway Bibles, a division of Good News Publishers. Used by permission. All rights reserved.

Cover design by Koechel Peterson & Associates, Inc., Minneapolis, Minnesota

Published in association with the literary agency of Wolgemuth & Associates.

HOW TO IMPACT AND INFLUENCE OTHERS
Copyright © 2002, 2008, 2011 by James Merritt
Published by Harvest House Publishers
Eugene, Oregon 97402
www.harvesthousepublishers.com

Library of Congress Cataloging-in-Publication Data
    Merritt, James Gregory
    How to impact and influence others / James Merritt.
        p. cm.
    Rev. ed. of: How to be a winner and influence anybody. c2002.
    ISBN 978-0-7369-2991-2 (pbk.)
    1. Leadership. 2. Influence (Psychology) I. Merritt, James Gregory, 1952- How to be a winner and influence anybody. II. Title.
    HD57.7.M47 2011
    650.1'3—dc22

                                                2010021575

All rights reserved. No part of this publication may be reproduced, stored in a retrieval system, or transmitted in any form or by any means—electronic, mechanical, digital, photocopy, recording, or any other—except for brief quotations in printed reviews, without the prior permission of the publisher.

Printed in the United States of America

11 12 13 14 15 16 17 18 19 / BP-SK / 10 9 8 7 6 5 4

To my mentor and hero in the faith,
Dr. Adrian Rogers

Contents

Acknowledgments

There are so many people to thank when one writes a book. Even though there may be only one author, good books are collaborative efforts with great teams standing with the author. I want to acknowledge that team.

First of all, I thank my agents, Robert and Eric Wolgemuth at Wolgemuth and Associates, for believing in me enough to represent me. I love that you are not only professionals, but also men of integrity and great character. It has been an honor to work with you, and I look forward to more collaboration.

I thank my editor, Rod Morris. You have a gentle yet firm way of telling me when things are bad—and I gave you many opportunities to tell me that! Thank you so much for working with me and being honest. It was a pleasure.

I thank Harvest House Publishers for allowing me to become a part of your family. Everyone has been a pleasure and joy to work with. You do things right. I am honored to entrust this project to the Harvest House team.

I am grateful for the church I pastor, Cross Pointe, and the staff I serve with. Ministering alongside great men and women of God has sharpened the virtues I describe in this book. I am grateful to the Lord to be both your pastor and fellow-worker with God.

This book would not even have come to pass had it not been for the urging and encouraging of my precious son, Jonathan. It is one thing to have ordinary people believe in you, but when your own son believes in you to the extent that Jonathan does, it humbles me beyond words. All three of my sons are my best friends, and I love them all, but I especially thank Jonathan for believing in his dad, admonishing me when I got discouraged in this project, and helping me to make this book as sharp as it could be. He is a writer far greater in ability than I ever hope to be, and I have learned so much from him. Jonathan, with all my heart, son, I love you and thank you for getting me to this point.

Finally, the greatest decision I ever made in my life—next to trusting Jesus Christ as my Lord and Savior—was marrying my wife, Teresa. Humanly speaking, you are the light of my life. I can't imagine a minute without you. You really are the finest person I've ever known. I am glad that God brought you into my life, and I will love you now, forever, and for always!

Introduction

Do you believe in the power of one? Not just the number but the power that number represents? Do you believe that one idea or one moment can be powerful? What about one person? If so, do you believe you might be that *one?* I do. You have the God-given potential to use your influence to impact others, shape futures, change lives, and make an eternal difference.

I have seen and experienced how seemingly ordinary people can use their influence to make a powerful impact. You have that same potential. We all do.

One solitary individual has the potential to affect those he meets in such a way that their lives are exponentially blessed and enhanced beyond the ordinary. Doubt that one person can make a difference?

- Winston Churchill convinced England they could survive the Nazi war machine, and they did.

- Vince Lombardi turned the Green Bay Packers from NFL doormats into legendary champions.

- Lee Iacocca turned Chrysler around and saved the company.

- Rosa Parks took a stand on a bus in Montgomery, Alabama, that eventually compelled the most powerful nation on earth to enforce true racial equality after almost two centuries of neglect.

- Florence Nightingale, the mother of modern nursing, transformed the care of patients by emphasizing sanitary design and hygiene in hospitals, practices that carry over to today.

- Do you think that George Washington, Abraham Lincoln, Susan B. Anthony, Marie Curie, Helen Keller, and Mother Teresa made a difference?

Still not convinced? We are often convinced that our votes don't count. Voter apathy sets in when the "I'm only one vote" mind-set sets in. The next time an election rolls around consider the difference that just one vote can make. It just so happens that one person, casting one vote, made the following differences in history.

- In 1645, one vote gave Oliver Cromwell control of England.

- In 1649, one vote caused Charles I of England to be executed.

- In 1776, one vote gave America the English language instead of German (thank God for that).

- In 1845, one vote brought Texas into the union.

- In 1868, one vote saved President Andrew Johnson from impeachment.

- In 1875, one vote changed France from a monarchy to a republic.

- In 1876, one vote gave Rutherford B. Hayes the United States presidency.

- In 1941, one vote saved the Selective Service System just twelve weeks before Pearl Harbor.[1]

In 1842, Henry Shoemaker worked as a hired hand on a farm in Indiana. Election day came and he remembered that he had promised his vote to Madison Marsh, a Democrat running for state representative. Though he had many other important things to do, he kept his promise. He rode his horse to the polling place and cast his ballot. Later it became known that Madison Marsh was elected *by one vote.*

During those years, state legislators elected U.S. senators. In January 1843, Indiana lawmakers convened for just such an election. During the sixth ballot, Marsh changed his vote, electing Democrat Edward Hannegan to the U.S. Senate *by one vote.*

Three years later, the United States Senate was considering a declaration of war on Mexico. There was a stalemate, and progress was not within sight until the legislature called the absent Senator Hannegan. He cast his vote in favor of war, and the scales tipped.

As a result of one hired hand in Indiana, two men were elected to office, and America went to war with Mexico. One man named Henry Shoemaker unknowingly exerted power to determine destiny and war.[2]

One person with just one idea can set off a chain reaction of other ideas that can change the course of history. A person with a sticky idea can effect political tsunamis, start wars, and even alter the way human beings view themselves and others.

In the early nineteenth century, Ludwig Feuerbach came up with the idea that rather than God being the creator of humanity,

humanity created the idea of God out of a psychological need to believe in a higher power. For years that idea got little traction until Karl Marx adopted it into his own thinking and expanded it to the idea in his famous dictum, "Religion is the opiate of the people." He was the first person to offer a popular materialist interpretation of history.

> One person with just one idea can set off a chain reaction
> of other ideas that can change the course of history.

Using that same idea, Charles Darwin later published his seminal work, *On the Origin of Species by Means of Natural Selection*. Darwin gave an explanation of the existence of all things apart from a divine creator, which challenged every former assumption about the origin of the universe and the creation of the human race.

Later a Jewish scientist by the name of Sigmund Freud used the religion-as-opiate idea to assert that religion often gives rise to mental illness and does more harm than good. He claimed that what had traditionally been called "sin" is actually a man-made taboo arising from incest and cannibalism.[3]

What's the point? One person can have such influence on others that it can transcend all boundaries, whether cultural, geographical, racial, or social. In addition to Freud, Darwin, Marx, and Feuerbach, choirs of people in every age have shaped history with their ideas.

Don't talk yourself out of believing that you also can make a difference. Your last name doesn't have to be Washington, Parks, or Lincoln to make a difference. Everybody was a nobody once. Education doesn't matter nearly as much as you might think. Bill

Gates doesn't have a college degree. Wealth doesn't determine influence either. Abraham Lincoln was poor most of his life.

I am not implying that you will one day be president of the United States, a TV star like Oprah, or a multimillionaire. I am not guaranteeing that masses of people will be clamoring for your autograph or following you on Twitter. I'm not promising that you will have 5000 friends on Facebook. I *am* saying that you are an appointment not an accident, and that you have within you the inborn potential to have an incredibly positive influence on the lives of others. You can have an impact that will outlive you and outlast you long after you have left this earth.

Everybody is talking about "going green" today. It seems like more and more people are concerned with their "ecological footprint." No matter which side of the issue you are on, everybody is talking about depletion of natural resources, recycling, reliance on fossil fuels, climate change, and the problem of pollution. One thing everyone can agree on is that we ought to leave as small an environmental footprint as possible as long as doing so is reasonable and doesn't put an undue burden on society.

> We should also be asking, "How can we increase our personal footprint?"

Everybody can agree that we should be good stewards of our planet because it doesn't belong to us. We don't own this world; we are just stewards of this world, and good stewardship says that we ought to take care of the creation God has given us. Even though we should be looking for ways to decrease our ecological footprint, we should also be asking, "How can we increase our personal footprint?"

I want you to imagine your life is like sand on a beach. Every day you leave a footprint in that sand. How long will your footprints last? Where will your footprints lead? Will you live in such a way that anyone who chooses to follow in your footsteps will be better for it, will be moved to reach their full potential, and perhaps most importantly, will themselves be able to make a greater more lasting impact on the people they meet? The poet Henry Wadsworth Longfellow put it this way:

> Lives of great men all remind us
> We can make our lives sublime
> And, departing, leave behind us
> Footprints on the sands of time.

Let's fast-forward for just a moment. Imagine that you have come to the end of your life. You have just checked out of your bodily hotel and entered into your final and eternal residence. Think about these two questions:

1. What one thing would you want said about you at your funeral?[4]

2. What epitaph would you want on your tombstone?

I have attended many funerals in my life (as you can imagine in my profession), but one in particular profoundly affected me, and I was not the officiating minister. The funeral was for Adrian Rogers. For 33 years, he was pastor of Bellevue Baptist Church in Memphis, Tennessee—a church that grew to 27,000 members under his tenure.

Dr. Rogers was the greatest preacher I have ever heard. He was funny with a quick wit. Many joked that his voice sounded just like God's voice would if you ever heard it, and his messages were filled with great illustrations, practical anecdotes, and tremendous wisdom.

When I was 30 years old, I was pastoring my first full-time church in Mississippi after graduating from seminary. I had never met Dr. Rogers, but I had heard him on tape and prayed that someday I might preach as well as he. I wrote him asking if he would give me an hour of his time if I made the 300-mile trek to Memphis. I was unconvinced that I'd even receive a response, but to my surprise, he invited me up on a Thursday to hear him speak at a businessmen's luncheon.

Filled with millions of butterflies, I made the drive to Memphis where I sat spellbound by another masterpiece message, and then he invited me to what I thought would be a formal one-hour meeting. I wish I had a picture of my face when we were ushered into a private dining area for a one-on-one lunch where I learned that this busy pastor of one of the largest churches in America *had reserved the entire afternoon for me*! For nearly five hours I learned more about preaching, sermon preparation, and leadership than I learned in six years at seminary.

Adrian Rogers's fingerprint is still on me. I've been told that people can see and hear his influence in my preaching, thinking, and approach to my work. I've dedicated this book to him. He may have left this earth years ago, but his impact and influence live on in my life every single day. You might say I'm living proof of the power of one.

This book is designed to help you experience that kind of impact on others as well. Each chapter offers you a unique approach to becoming a "power-of-one person." A power-of-one person understands that what a person *is* will leave a far greater impact on others in the long run than what a person *does*. The emphasis in this book is not *conduct* as much as it is *character*.

You will find nine character traits that together form a matrix for a lasting and positive impact on others. Each chapter includes at the end an action you can take to begin to see your influence take shape in your personal interactions.

> I can't do anything about your heritage, and neither can you. But you can do something about your legacy.

I realize there will be those reading these words who believe that their past mistakes or their family heritage have spoiled their chances. You think you have already blown it, and your influence factor and impact ledger are completely negative. Perhaps divorce, alcoholism, growing up in a dysfunctional family, public shame, even incarceration colors your family portrait or has left scars on your life.

I can't do anything about your heritage, and neither can you. But you can do something about your legacy. You cannot change your past, but you can do a lot about your future. Beginning today, you can become a power-of-one person. Believe that you have within you the God-given potential and commensurate power to influence others in such a way that you make in them a life-changing difference.

Perhaps this final story can help you see this in high definition. Edwin Booth died with a letter in his pocket that reminds us of how anybody, anywhere, anytime can use his or her personal influence to make an eternal difference. At one time, Edwin Booth was considered by many to be the greatest actor in the world. He had a magnificent voice and a passionate style, and he owned the theater. His career was taking off until a fatal shooting took place in April 1865. That was when his brother, John Wilkes, assassinated President Abraham Lincoln.

The stigma of that single act drove Edwin into seclusion and retirement. He knew for the rest of his life that whenever anyone heard the name Booth, they would think of John Wilkes. The family name had been forever tainted by his brother's deed.

However, Edwin Booth's legacy turned out to be not one of death and disappointment but of life and influence. During a busy event in the Jersey City, New Jersey, train station, Edwin was standing near a young man who lost his footing on the platform and nearly fell on the tracks next to a moving train. Without hesitation, Edwin rescued this young man by reaching down to pull him up by the collar.

There was just a brief exchange of gratitude, and Edwin never dreamed how significant that moment would become. Weeks later he received a letter from Ulysses Grant's chief secretary. It was a letter of thanks for his heroic deed, because the life that Edwin Booth had saved was Robert Todd Lincoln, the son of Abraham Lincoln.

Edwin Booth took Grant's letter to the grave, because it was a reminder that we may not be able to change our heritage, but we can change our legacy.[5]

I am determined to leave behind the greatest legacy I possibly can. I want you to join me in that pursuit.

Chapter One

The Killer App

*"The loneliest place in the world is the
human heart when love is absent."*

AUTHOR UNKNOWN

S itting in a cold hospital room, you play with the frayed
strings on the edge of your shirt. You're trying to occupy
your mind, pretending not to be nervous for the sake of
your wife. Suddenly, the latch clicks and the door swings open.

"I'm going to give it to you straight," your doctor says. "You
have only a few days to live."

The doctor says his prognosis is certain. No chance for error,
no possibility the files were mixed. No cure. No antidote. No
treatment. Nothing. Your ticket for the train to eternity has
been punched, and you will be at the station on time whether
you like it or not.

May I suggest that the most important thing in your life
will not be the bottom line of your balance sheet, the size of
your portfolio, the number of people who reported to you, the
title you carried at your company, the size of your pension, or
the letters behind your name on your business card. The one
thing that *will* leap to the top of your priority list will be relationships.

A recent Harris Poll asked many Americans to name what they considered most important in life. Consider their response.

- Relationships—56 percent
- Religious faith—21 percent
- Making the world a better place—12 percent
- A fulfilling career—5 percent
- Money—5 percent

Respondents to this poll ranked relationships higher in importance than either career or money by a ratio of more than *10 to 1*. While it could be debated that not everyone in the survey responded truthfully, at least the poll reveals what, deep down, people know is truly important.

John Donne was right: "No man is an island, entire of itself; every man is a piece of the continent, a part of the main...any man's death diminishes me, because I am involved in mankind; and therefore never send to know for whom the bell tolls; it tolls for thee."

Think about how crucial relationships are:

- A successful marriage depends upon the *relationship* between the husband and wife.
- A happy home depends upon the *relationship* between the parents and the children (and between the siblings).
- A prosperous business depends upon the *relationship* between the employees and the customers.
- A peaceful community depends upon the *relationship* between neighbors.

- A successful political campaign depends upon the *relationship* between the candidate and the voters.

- A stable nation depends upon the *relationship* between nations.

Everyone needs someone. Even Batman needed Robin. Variety may give life spice, but *relationships* give life significance, purpose, and meaning.

That principle will help you to understand and appreciate something John Rockefeller once said. In his day, Rockefeller was the richest man in the world. Accounting for inflation, he was far wealthier than Bill Gates is today. A business mind *par excellence*, Rockefeller once said, "The ability to deal with people is as purchasable a commodity as sugar or coffee, and I will pay more for the ability than any other under the sun."

> Variety may give life spice, but *relationships* give life significance, purpose, and meaning.

Rockefeller's words still ring true today. Who you are in the core of your being and how you relate to others will be more valuable at the end of life's journey than the political acumen of Bill Clinton, the wealth of Oprah Winfrey, the fame of Tiger Woods, or the influence of Barack Obama.

No one on earth has the power to influence the people you know more than you do. If you can harness and control your relationships, you will possess incredible power. That's one of the principles that makes this book so different. Other books discuss the "how" of relationship building, networking, influencing, and ultimately leading; this book deals with the "who."

If you want to have the maximum influence and the greatest impact on others, you must believe that *who you are matters more than what you do*.

Over the last several years, a debate has raged in this country over whether character really counts or ability is all that matters. The consensus appears to be that a person's behavior in private has little bearing on his or her ability to lead or influence in public. Yet this belief contradicts public sentiment.

A core of character exists within us that, if activated and lived out, enables us to achieve the greatest possible impact on others. One of the biggest components of our character is the subject of this chapter. This component is the most powerful emotion and experience in the world. When expressed, it can forge new partnerships or destroy dreams.

In German, *Ich liebe dich*.

In Mandarin, *Wo ai ni*.

In Japanese, *Sukiyo*.

In Russian, *Ya tyebya lyublyu*.

In Greek, *S'agapo*.

In Spanish, *Te amo*.

In Polish, *Kocham cie*.

In English, *I love you*.

The Best App You'll Ever Add to Your iLife

I recently broke down after much resistance and joined the other six billion people of the world and bought an iPhone. I previously owned a "crackberry," and I was frankly very pleased with it. What pushed me over the edge to make the switch? The applications. Everyone knows that the iPhone apps are killer cool. Today, as a proud iPhone user, I visit my neighborhood Apple store at least once a week to see what new apps have been released.

If life were an iPhone, love would be
the first app you should add.

Tim Sanders wrote a tremendous book with an amazing title: *Love Is the Killer App: How to Win Business and Influence Friends.* He states that love is the crucial element in the search for personal and professional success. According to Sanders, if life were an iPhone, love would be the first app you should add.

From everything I've learned, Sanders is onto something. I am convinced that the greatest leaders are loving leaders—their followers, friends, and employees know that the one above them always has their best interests at heart. Stop and think about this: Would you say that the people who had the greatest and most lasting impact on you were people you felt genuinely loved you and cared for you?

I've studied love a lot over the years. My mentor on this topic knows more about love than anyone in history. You've probably heard of Him: Jesus. Even non-Christians agree that Jesus knew something about loving others. He taught about it, but most importantly, He lived it. In fact, Jesus gave the greatest, most succinct explanations of love ever recorded:

> One of them, an expert in the law, tested him with this question: "Teacher, which is the greatest commandment in the Law?"
>
> Jesus replied: "'Love the Lord your God with all your heart and with all your soul and with all your mind.' This is the first and greatest commandment. And the second is like it: 'Love your neighbor as yourself.' All the Law and the Prophets hang on these two commandments" (Matthew 22:35-40).

This sounds good, but how do love and influence interface? Why is love such a crucial component of an influencer's toolkit? To answer these questions, I propose we delve into Jesus' words. No matter your religious tradition, no one denies that Jesus was a person of profound influence and impact even two millennia after His life. I am convinced that if Jesus were alive today, He would be teaching aspiring influencers everywhere how to love others and impact the world.

Love Is a Must

Jesus' love is a command not a request. This command clues us in about the true nature and behavior of love. If love can be commanded, then it cannot be merely emotional—only a matter of feelings—as is often portrayed in the entertainment industry. That may be an accurate depiction of juvenile ardor, but genuine love is much more than a mere feeling. Love is a matter of the will. That's why Jesus is able to command us to express it. It's a commandment followed by a commitment. Although feelings are important, true love functions regardless of feelings.

For thousands of years (and to this day in some Eastern cultures), parents arranged their children's marriages. Many brides and bridegrooms never saw each other until their wedding day.

A certain young lady from India was to be married to a young man she had never met. One day she received a letter from her fiancé to acquaint her with him prior to the wedding. But the young woman returned the letter unopened, saying she believed love should be developed after marriage and not before. "When we are born," the woman said, "we cannot choose our mother and father or our brothers and sisters. Yet we learn to live with them and to love them. So it is with our husband or wife." In societies that accept such a philosophy, divorce is almost non-existent.

While I do not suggest that we return to the practice of arranged marriages, I do insist that "romantic love" as popularly understood has little to do with a successful marriage. Love is more than feelings.

My marriage is a perfect example of this. I have been married for over three decades. I proposed to my wife and told her I "loved her" on our second date. I actually experienced "love at first sight," but I thought the first date might be rushing it a bit, and I wanted to give her time to get used to the idea that she loved me too. Did I *really* love her after only two dates? I can honestly say that I loved her as much as anyone can after only two days of interaction. But my love then was galaxies away from the real love I have for her today.

Thirty years later, I understand that love is a choice rather than a sappy let's-all-hold-hands-and-sing "We Are The World" sentiment. Love is a commitment to caring for others and doing for others regardless of our feelings. We choose to love.

Mark Sanborn in his wonderful little book *The Fred Factor* made this observation:

> I learned a long time ago that liking people and loving them are different. Liking someone is an emotional response. Unlike love, "like" is a feeling. The tough part is that we can't control our emotions. We can control how we choose to express those emotions but not the feelings themselves. A healthy person can choose to be angry and still choose to act lovingly...A feeling is a reaction. Maybe that's one reason Jesus didn't say "Like your enemies." He knew that liking or not liking someone was not always in our immediate control...I

have learned that love is, among other things, an action. I can love someone I don't necessarily like. I can do something or act toward that person in a certain way because I know it is the right thing to do even if I don't feel warm and fuzzy doing it.[1]

Those of you who are managers and leaders would do well to remember that. You may not like your employees, but if you stop loving them, you've gone too far. Your boss may not be likeable, but you must do your best to love him or her despite this sentiment. Jesus commanded us to love, and taking His words seriously makes us better leaders and influencers.

Love Has an Upward Dimension

Real love is multidimensional. In the passage in Matthew, Jesus reveals three directions for love: toward God, others, and ourselves. The first love—for God—is an upward love that must take priority. We should love God first, most, and best. Jesus tells us that God deserves all of our love, not only part of our love. We should love no one more than God. Jesus taught that if love is to be fully manifested, maximally beneficial, and mutually satisfying, we should love God first, others second, and ourselves last.

Some readers may squirm in discomfort at this juncture and prefer to leave any reference to deity out of the influencer equation. This is neither completely possible nor desirable. Love for God *only enhances* our love for others and hence strengthens our ability to influence and impact others in a positive way.

You might be asking, "Is it possible to love others or to experience love apart from God?" Certainly, for people do it every day. But if Jesus was right, unless we first love God and receive His love, we can't fully experience or manifest the greatest love.

If you love God, your love for others will grow even greater, for this upward love supernaturally produces a love for others.

> Love is like a river—it always flows *downstream*. When the vertical dimension of love is experienced, the horizontal dimension will be a natural result.

When you love God the most, you will love others the best. British author C.S. Lewis once said, "When I have learned to love God better than my earthly dearest, I shall love my earthly dearest better than I do now." Indeed love is like a river—it always flows *downstream*. When the vertical dimension of love is experienced, the horizontal dimension will be a natural result.

Love Has an Outward Dimension

Jesus also calls us to love our neighbor. A love for God inescapably motivates a love for others. Of course, it's hard to love everybody. As C.W. Vanderbergh wrote, "To love the whole world for me is no chore. My only real problem is my neighbor next door."

Most businesses would benefit greatly if the boss truly loved his employees and they knew it. Most marriages would be happier if spouses heard and saw constant reminders that they were loved. Most families would be happier if the parents constantly and lovingly affirmed their children.

Consider this simple but powerful principle that can transform any relationship almost overnight: *When it comes to love, say it.*

My dad went to heaven more than 10 years ago. He grew up in a relatively good—but loveless—home. Between them, my grandparents lived a total of 180 years. In the combined 106 years my dad knew them, they never once told him they loved him. I am so glad that the last time I saw my dad alive, I told him, "You are my best man and I love you."

About 20 years ago I met Tony, a Palestinian who has since become a part of my family. Until I told him "I love you," he had never heard another man say those three words to him. At first, all he could say was "thank you." I just kept on speaking those three words. After years of telling him, he said to me, "I love you, man." Later he told me that he has never felt so good about expressing his love to others in such an open way.

Why not start now to become a loving person or a person better at loving? For the next 30 days, try the following:

- Tell every member of your family that you love them, and give them several loving touches, pats, hugs, and kisses every day.

- If you are a boss, manager, or employer, tell your employees that you love and appreciate them for the work they do. Find some way to give a tangible expression (note, card, or pat on the back) of your loving affirmation.

- If you are an employee, do the same for your employers.

- If you have been at odds with someone, go to that person and affirm your love for him, regardless of your differences.

One word of warning: loving others and expressing that love verbally and tangibly can entail great risk. But the risk is worth taking. I can name at least four reasons why those three words need to come from our lips regularly and often: (1) you need to say it; (2) you need to hear yourself say it; (3) others need to hear you say it; and (4) you need to hear it from others. What's wrong with a general telling his troops he loves them? Why doesn't a boss tell his employees he loves them? Why shouldn't a coach tell his players he loves them? In my mind, they should.

In 1999, Duke University played the University of Connecticut for the NCAA men's basketball championship. Duke had a chance to win, but in the last five seconds a Duke player lost the ball and, with it, the game.

What did Coach Mike Krzyzewski say after he lost for the fourth time in a national championship game? "I'm really proud of my team," he declared. "I really love these guys. I have a hard time being sad. I don't coach for winning. I coach for relationships." Coach K really does love his players, and people know it. That's one reason why he is considered one of the outstanding coaches and recruiters in America.

Husbands, your wife needs to hear you say those three words, repeatedly, every day. Don't be like the husband and wife who were sitting on a swing one afternoon. The woman turned to her spouse and said, "You never tell me you love me." Without looking at his wife, the man dryly replied, "I told you 37 years ago that I loved you, and if I change my mind, I will let you know."

Your spouse may *know* it, but they still need to hear it.

> If love is going to be maximally effective,
> it should be seen, heard, and felt.

But saying it isn't enough. There's another action piece at work here: *When it comes to love, show it.* Love must not only be articulated but also demonstrated. Love is proactive, practical, and personal. It is tangible—something to be seen as well as heard. If love is going to be maximally effective, it should be seen, heard, and felt.

A simple touch can convey an incredible sense of love, affirmation, and acceptance. A study conducted at UCLA several years ago found that to maintain physical and emotional health, men and women need eight to ten meaningful touches each day. These researchers defined meaningful touch as a gentle tap, stroke, kiss, or hug, given by a "significant other" such as a husband, wife, parent, or close friend. Of course, in a professional relationship (and in certain personal relationships), caution should be exercised in touching anyone of the opposite sex. The point is, love should be tangibly expressed in the right place and time.

An old commercial appropriately asked parents, "Have you hugged your kids today?" Good coaches high-five their players, good husbands hug their wives, and good bosses give employees encouraging pats on the back as a way of expressing loving affirmation. It may sound trite but a "pat on the back" really can be beneficial.

Dr. Dolores Krieger, professor of nursing at New York University, has done numerous studies on the effect of human touch. She found that both the toucher and the one being touched receive great physiological benefit. Here's how: Red blood cells carry hemoglobin, a substance that carries oxygen to the body's tissues. Dr. Krieger found that hemoglobin levels in the bloodstreams of both people increase when one lays hands on the other. As hemoglobin levels rise, body tissues receive more oxygen. This oxygen increase invigorates both parties and can even aid in the healing process (the healing power of love in action).

An incredible true story illustrates this power of a loving touch. Leprosy patients feel no physical pain except in the early stages of the disease. Lack of feeling is the problem, for after leprosy bacilli deaden nerve cells, patients lose pain as an all-important danger signal. They may step on a rusty nail or scratch an infected spot on the eyeball without even knowing it. The result can be the eventual loss of a limb or vision, but at no point does the leprosy patient actually hurt.

Although they do not feel physical pain, leprosy patients do suffer incredibly from the rejection of the outside world. Dr. Paul Brand, a leprosy specialist, tells of a bright young man he treated in India. In the course of his examination, he laid his hand on the patient's shoulder and informed him through a translator about the treatment he would receive. To the doctor's shock, the man began to tremble and sob uncontrollably. Brand immediately asked the translator what he had done wrong. She quizzed the patient and explained, "No, doctor. He says he is crying because you put your hand around his shoulder. Until he came here, no one had touched him in many years." Dr. Brand expressed love for this man, and it translated into both influence and impact.

The law says, "What's mine is mine; I'll keep it."

Our lust says, "What's yours is mine; I'll take it."

True love says, "What's mine is yours; I'll share it."

Love sets off a divine chain reaction. Love is the spark that kindles the fire of compassion. Compassion is the fire that lights the candle of service. Service is the candle that ignites the torch of hope. Hope is the torch that lights the beacon of faith. Faith is the beacon that reflects the power of God. And God is the power that creates the miracle of love.

The way of love is not only the right way; it is the best way.

You can experience nothing as self-gratifying or encouraging as loving others through both words and deeds.

Love Has an Inward Dimension

Many forget that Jesus said we should love our neighbors *as ourselves*. On the surface, this seems to be a mandate for self-love. But when we consider His words in context, we see the principle Jesus gave was radical and refreshing. Jesus declared that if we love God properly, we will come to love ourselves properly. The great Swiss psychologist Paul Tournier once said, "If a person will love God the way he ought to love God, he will then love others the way he ought to love others; and when he loves God and others the way they ought to be loved, he will never need a psychiatrist." Love can give you a healthy mental picture of yourself, enhancing the type of self-esteem that avoids self-worship or self-idolization.

The topics of self and self-esteem have generated an incredible amount of press in recent years. Much of the coverage has been counterproductive, fostering an unhealthy obsession with self and spawning a culture of selfishness that chants the mantra, "What's in it for me?" Simply affirming "I'm okay and you're okay" is not good enough, for neither you nor I may really be okay. If you are okay with God and okay with others, chances are you will be okay with yourself. When you love God and your neighbor, self won't seem so important. You will find that love can motivate in a way that fame or fortune never could.

> If you are not loving, you are not living.

If you wrestle with insecurities, self-doubt, even self-loathing, it will eventually be revealed in your relationships. Unless dealt with, these traits will greatly hinder your ability to impact and influence others. I have found that people who are irritable, hard to work with, or hard to get along with usually are most unhappy with themselves.

A wise writer and evangelist, Henry Drummond, once said:

> To love abundantly is to live abundantly; and to love forever is to live forever. Hence, eternal life is inextricably bound up with love. We want to live forever for the same reason we want to live tomorrow. Why do you want to live tomorrow? It is because someone loves you, and you want to see them tomorrow because you love them back. Being loved and loving others is the only reason why we should continue living. It is when a man has no one to love him, or thinks that he has no one to love him, that he commits suicide. So long as he has friends, those who love him and whom he loves, he will live; because to live is to love. [2]

Drummond was right. If you are not loving, you are not living. Even the poorest person on earth can give away love. We all need to be loved and we all need to love someone else, for someone always needs our love. I must warn you that a life of love is risky. Choosing to love makes you vulnerable. But that is the difference between losers and winners: *A winner is willing to risk not being like others to rise above others.* As author and poet William Arthur Ward says, "Only the person who risks is free."

The Gift That Keeps on Giving

Love involves risk, pain, and heartache, but it can bring a tidal wave of joy that washes the tough times away. David Ireland wrote *Letters to an Unborn Child* while dying from a crippling neurological disease. He composed these letters to the unborn child still in the womb of his wife—a child he knew he'd probably never see, hold, rock, kiss, or take to a ball game or a movie. A child he might never shoot baskets with, take to the circus, or comfort after a bad dream. He desperately wanted that child to know that, whether dead or alive, "Daddy loves his son or daughter." With that in mind, David wrote the following:

> Your mother is special. Few men know what it's like to receive appreciation for taking their wives out to dinner when it entails what it does for us. It means that she has to dress me, shave me, brush my teeth, comb my hair, wheel me out of the house and down the steps, open the garage and put me in the car, take the pedals off the chair, stand me up, sit me in the seat of the car, twist me around so that I'm comfortable, fold the wheelchair, put it in the car, go around to the other side of the car, start it up, back it out, get out of the car, pull the garage door down, get back into the car, and drive off to the restaurant.
>
> And then, it starts all over again; she gets out of the car, unfolds the wheelchair, opens the door, spins me around, stands me up, seats me in the wheelchair, pushes the pedals out, closes and locks the car, wheels me into the restaurant, then takes the pedals off the wheelchair so I won't be uncomfortable. We sit down to have dinner, and she feeds me through the entire meal. And when it's over she pays the bill, pushes the wheelchair out to the car again and reverses the same routine.
>
> And when it's over—finished—with real warmth she'll say, "Honey, thank you for taking me out to dinner." I never quite know how to answer.[3]

I have never met this tremendous woman, but I guarantee you she knows how to impact and influence *anybody*. I want her on my team anytime! Even while her husband was dying, she kept him *really* living by her loving. Risky? Yes. Difficult? Absolutely. Yet she teaches us all that the greatest rewards in life come when we love and are loved.

Like Ireland's wife, we too have been given the task of loving. We must learn to love God, others, and ourselves in the proper proportions and order. It is risky, but it's worth it. And it will pay dividends from the bank of influence and impact for years to come.

> **Principle One—** *Love:* Make sure someone sees it, hears it, or feels it from you every day, either by telling them or showing them.

Chapter Two

Joy Ride

"You can't do much about the length of your life,
but you can do a lot about its depth and width."

AUTHOR UNKNOWN

Laughing is one of the best parts of life. It is such good medicine that it can relieve stress, cure headaches, fight infections, and even alleviate hypertension. Laughing produces well-documented physical benefits similar to those obtained through vigorous physical exercise. When you tip your head back and cackle aloud, muscles in the abdomen, chest, shoulders, and elsewhere contract, while the heart rate and blood pressure increase. In one burst of this activity, the pulse can double from 60 to 120, while systolic blood pressure can shoot from a normal 120 to 200. Once laughing ceases, heartbeat and blood pressure dip below normal—a sign of reduced stress.

Laughter is good for you and laughter brings health—a fact that was known by wise King Solomon: "A cheerful heart is good medicine" (Proverbs 17:22). That really is more than a verse of Scripture—it's also a medical statement, as we just saw. When merriness fills the tanks of our hearts, we feel better on the inside.

Joy and Happiness: Not Siamese Twins

Don't confuse happiness with merriness. Merriness comes from joy, not from happiness. Understanding this is crucial to your emotional well-being as well as your influence on others. There are times we cannot and should not be happy—when people are hurting, going through tragedy, losing jobs or loved ones. In the face of injustice, happiness is inappropriate if not impossible. Yet, in a real sense we should always remain joyful. We cannot be happy without being joyful, but we can be joyful without being happy.

This is a key point that you must not miss. Jesus said to His disciples, "I have told you this so that my joy may be in you and that your joy may be complete" (John 15:11). The Great Rabbi makes it plain that the joy He is speaking of is unique ("my joy") and fulfilling in a way that the world's happiness is not ("that your joy may be complete"). Jesus makes clear that being a faithful follower of His teaching brings one an inner joy that is real and resilient regardless of economic indicators, interest rates, government deficits, or the triumvirate of pestilence, disease, and death.

> We cannot be happy without being joyful,
> but we can be joyful without being happy.

How can this be? He had just told them previously that they enjoyed a love that transcends all others—the love of a heavenly Father that is unconditionally offered and, once accepted, permanently experienced (John 15:9-10). Nothing can compare to the love of God. His love is not based on looks, personality, wealth, or even moral goodness. It is offered without any preconditions and is neither fickle nor failing. You can't do anything to make God love you more, and you can do nothing to make God love you less.

Furthermore, divine love doesn't just give you warm fuzzies; it is constantly at work to direct you to make wise decisions, protect you from making poor decisions, and even correct you when you make bad decisions. God's love guarantees acceptance when all others have rejected you, forgiveness when all others judge you, and mercy when all others want to condemn you. When you bask in this love, you bathe in a wellspring of joy bubbling up in your heart. Nothing and no one should be able to take this away from you.

I called a dear friend of mine the day I wrote this chapter because the date represented one of the saddest days of his life. Twenty years ago his 23-year-old son was killed in a motorcycle accident. As I called him to let him know I was thinking of him, I couldn't help but think of how full of joy my friend is every day. I said, "Ken, I'm writing a chapter on the necessity of being a joy-filled person, and I was wondering how you've maintained your joy all these years?"

Ken thought for a moment and said through tears and a breaking voice, "I came to understand quickly that even though grief can rob you of your happiness, it cannot rob you of a joy that is far deeper and stronger. Even in the terrible moment when I landed and was met with this devastating news, I was simultaneously strengthened by my faith, which helped me see the big picture."

He took a deep breath and continued. "I knew that Paul was not suffering, and I would see him again. We had enjoyed a great father-son relationship. We had a love for each other that death could not end, and I had a wife and two loving daughters who adored me, and a faith that had prepared me for this moment. I can't explain it, but even in the most difficult of times, I had a joy in my heart that helped me smile on the inside even through the tears on the outside."

Listening to Ken, I was reminded of the contrasts between joy and happiness. Consider these distinctions:

- Happiness is external; joy is internal.

- Happiness depends on outward circumstances; joy depends on inward character.

- Happiness depends on what happens to us; joy depends on who lives within us.

- Happiness is based on chance; joy is based on choice.

> Happiness is temporary and fickle;
> joy is permanent and settled.

The word *happiness* comes from the old English word *happ*, which literally means "chance." It corresponds to the Latin *fortuna*, which means "luck." These words suggest that if things happen the way we want them to happen, then we are happy. But if they don't happen the way we want, we are unhappy. Happiness is temporary and fickle; joy is permanent and settled.

Created for Joy

Unfortunately, many people think God is some type of cosmic killjoy who frowns at smiles, cringes at laughter, and hates anything that smacks of joy and delight. Yet, as C.S. Lewis noted, "Joy is the serious business of heaven." And as we just saw, the person universally accepted as the greatest teacher who ever lived said His teachings were not just for information but for transformation—to bring a joy that would be permanent and complete.

Indeed, the Bible is one of the most joy-filled books ever written! It might surprise some to learn that the Bible uses the words *joy* and *joyful* some 245 times. The word *rejoice* appears 150 times. The Bible instructs us to be joyful and rejoice nearly 400 times.

It might seem odd that God tells us to experience joy, but that fact illustrates the difference between joy and happiness. Joy sometimes just happens when good things unfold for us. No doubt we may feel joy when, as the song from the musical *Oklahoma* declares, "Everything's going my way." But it is important to note that *joy is also a choice.*

You can choose to be joyful regardless of your circumstances.

Let me tell you a secret about joy that differentiates it even more from happiness: More than an emotion, joy is an attitude. Emotions cannot be chosen—no one can tell you to feel happy if you are not. But you can choose to be joyful regardless of your circumstances.

Imagine you are mired in a muck of unhappiness, and you go to a professional counselor and lie on the couch, spend tons of money, spend countless hours pouring out your unhappiness to him only to hear him say: "Don't worry, be happy!" You would probably be ready to take action to make him extremely unhappy! Telling someone to be happy is foolish, for happiness is not a choice.

Neither is it a commodity that can be bought. Too many people find out too late that money cannot buy happiness, much less joy. It has been wisely said that the poor are better off than the rich because the poor still think that money will buy happiness; the rich know better. Trying to find happiness or joy in material things is like drinking saltwater: the more you drink, the thirstier you get.

A well-dressed restaurant customer was staring sullenly into his drink. The waitress, trying to be kind, asked if something was wrong.

"Well, two months ago my grandfather died and left me $500,000 in oil wells."

"That doesn't sound like something to get upset about," the waitress said.

"Yeah," the young man said, "but last month my uncle passed away and left me $100,000 in stocks."

"So why are you sitting there so unhappy?"

"Because this month, so far, nobody's left me a cent!"

The great poet Horace wrote these words:

> Happy is the man and happy is he alone,
> He who can call today his own.
> He who is secure within can say,
> "Tomorrow do thy worst, for I have lived today."

Today is really all we have, and we can choose to be joyful today. We get to ride on the merry-go-round of life only once. Why not choose to enjoy the ride?

The Power of Joy

Joy gives us strength for living. It allows us to walk in the sunshine even when the rain pours down. It gives us wings to fly when most of the world is walking. It gives us strength to persevere even under the worst circumstances. Searching for a silver lining in every dark cloud is indeed far better than seeing a dark lining in every silver cloud.

Furthermore, joy "baits the hook" with the one thing people want most in this world: hope. Joy gives people a sense of optimism, hope, and merriment that endures with the times and doesn't evaporate with troubles. Even his political foes agreed that Ronald Reagan was one of the most well-liked presidents in our history. His sunny disposition radiated an infectious joy.

Human beings spend many of their waking hours seeking something to fill the emptiness in their souls. That something is joy, and if you can offer someone joy, you will be a winner and an influencer far beyond your wildest dreams. I once heard a friend say, "Joy is a winsome magnet that draws people in because it is the one thing they do not have."

Leaders pull everyone else around them up when they are down. Not only do they see the glass half-full, but they invest energy in the lives of those around them so that they keep a joyful perspective as well. If you are going to maximize your influence and leave a lasting impact on others, you must become contagious with joy. There are two practical ways to do this.

> Leaders pull everyone else around
> them up when they are down.

First, *create a joyful environment*. My wife loves to go to certain restaurants for what she calls the "atmosphere" or "ambience." The surroundings, the service, and the sounds create for her a relaxed and romantic feeling that you won't get at McDonald's. Leaders can create environments of joy so that others experience it and even catch it. It can be something as simple as walking around the office giving everyone a smile or a thumbs-up, or encouraging a mother and father to make sure fun is on the agenda every day in some way in the home.

Second, *invest in others*. When you share your life with another person, you can give him or her a "joy transfusion" even when times are tough. We really do have the power and ability to help people see that life is good in so many ways, that it is always full of potential, and that we have reasons to smile, laugh, and even give thanks for the many positives that are with us daily. Zig Ziglar has been a mentor and encourager to me. Many times he has called out of the blue with that bubbly joyful voice of his and breathed a joyful attitude into my life. Who will you become a mentor and encourager to? Choose to invest in others, and you'll unlock the power of joy.

The greatest secret of personal joy—and perhaps the one principle that will practically guarantee it—is this: *Give joy to others, and you will get it for yourself.* Helen Keller once wrote in her journal, "Many persons have a wrong idea of what constitutes happiness [and joy]. It is not attained through self-gratification but through fidelity to a worthy purpose."

Look around and you will find that the most joyful people are those who invest their time and energy in others. The unhappiest people are those who wait around, wondering how someone is going to make them happy. Someone once asked Karl Menninger, the great psychiatrist, how a lonely and unhappy person should deal with the unhappiness. "Lock the door behind you, go across the street, find someone who is hurting, and help him or her," he said.

Chief Enjoyment Officer

Dale Carnegie said the expression you wear on your face

is far more important than the clothes you wear on your back. Carnegie tells how a New York City department store—recognizing the pressures its salesclerks felt during the Christmas rush—presented its customers with the following philosophy:

> It costs nothing but creates much.
>
> It enriches those who receive without impoverishing those who give.
>
> It happens in a flash, and the memory of it lasts forever.
>
> None are so rich they can get along without it, and none so poor but are richer for its benefits.
>
> It creates happiness in the home, fosters goodwill in a business, and is the countersign of friends.
>
> It is rest to the weary, daylight to the discouraged, sunshine to the sad, and Nature's best antidote for trouble.
>
> Yet it cannot be bought, begged, borrowed, nor stolen, for it's no earthly good to anybody until it is given away.
>
> And if in the last-minute rush of Christmas buying some of our salespeople should be too tired to give you a smile, may we ask you to leave one of yours?
>
> For nobody needs a smile so much as those who have none left to give!

When I speak of smiling, I do not mean a forced smile that shows a cynical spirit. I mean a smile that naturally reveals a heart filled with joy. Joy is difficult, if not impossible, to conceal.

Some prospectors out in California once discovered a rich vein of gold; the strike would make them all instant millionaires. They had but one problem: they had not legally staked their claim. They made a solemn vow to one another that they would not tell a soul about the discovery until they had completed the legal work and bought all of the supplies and tools needed to begin digging. They went into town and divided their duties—some going to get food, others to get tools, and others to file the claim. But as they left, they noticed practically half the town was following them. At first each felt fury, believing one of them had betrayed the others. But when they asked how their discovery had leaked out, one of the townspeople replied, "It was the look of joy on your faces. We don't ever see that around here—and we knew it must be gold!" Joy and excitement so filled these men that their faces betrayed what was in their hearts.

As a leader you can be a CEO—Chief Enjoyment Officer—regardless of your official position.

The Journey to Joy

Think of life as a journey you can either endure or enjoy. Since you make the journey only once, you may as well enjoy the ride. But the ride begins when you establish a personal relationship with God, the ultimate source of all joy. This is the first step to experience joy that will stick and last a lifetime. The Bible says:

> You [God] have made known to me the path of life;
>   you will fill me with joy in your presence,
>   with eternal pleasures at your right hand.
>   (Psalm 16:11)

God made you for Himself, and only when you find His purpose for your life will you also find peace and joy.

If you were to take a fish out of the ocean and place it on the beach, you would watch its scales dry up as it gasped for breath. Is that fish full of joy? Absolutely not. If you covered it with a mountain of cash, would that make the fish joyful? No. Would a beach chair, an iPod, a good book, and some iced tea restore its joy? Of course not. Suppose you bought it a new wardrobe of double-breasted fins and people-skin shoes. Would that satisfy it? Obviously not.

Only one thing will restore joy to this fish: putting it back in the water. That fish can never have joy on the beach because it wasn't made for the beach, it was made for the ocean. In the same way, we were made for fellowship with God, and we will be like a fish out of water—never knowing the true source of everlasting joy—until we find it in Him.

The journey begins with God but continues with you. When you plug into God, He changes you into a person of joy. And as a person of joy, you must remember to be a grateful rather than a grumbling person. Gratitude is often the missing link in the chain that binds joy to the grind of everyday living. Grumbling and complaining not only take your focus off the positives; they drain the energy of joy from the battery of your heart. Stop and take notice of the simple things in life you can feel grateful for.

A man was sitting on a train, looking out the window as his railcar traveled through the countryside. Whenever the train passed open fields, he would say, "Wonderful." As it chugged through woods, the man would again say, "Wonderful." Everything he saw—cows grazing in a pasture, birds sitting on fences, or just ordinary buildings—would evoke an amazed look and an exclamation of "Wonderful."

Another man watched him for a while and then said, "Sir, why is everything so wonderful to you? I don't see the big deal." The man replied, "I'm sure you haven't understood. You see, I have been blind since birth, but I have just had an operation and now I can see—and to me, *everything* is wonderful!"

Be satisfied with what you do have; don't sour about what you don't have. Remember two words: *greed* and *envy.* These are guaranteed joy killers. A wise person knows that more is not necessarily better and that others are not necessarily better off. Even if the grass *is* greener on the other side, that just means it grows faster and is more difficult to cut.

> Remember two words: *greed* and *envy.*
> These are guaranteed joy killers.

A wealthy businessman felt disturbed to find a fisherman sitting lazily beside his boat. "Why aren't you out there fishing?" he asked.

"Because I've caught enough fish for today," the man replied.

"Why don't you catch more fish than you need?" the rich man asked.

"What would I do with them?"

"You could earn more money and buy a better boat so you could go deeper and catch more fish. You could purchase nylon nets, catch even more fish, and make more money. Soon you would have a fleet of boats and be rich like me."

"Then what would I do?" the fisherman asked.

"You could sit down and enjoy life," the rich man said.

The fisherman looked peacefully across the water, smiled, and said, "What do you think I'm doing *now?*"

That fisherman had learned the secret of enjoying life.

Don't Miss Out

Life is too short to miss out on the joy of knowing God, serving others, and delighting in becoming a blessing to others. Make the decision now to go through life with a smile on your face, a smile that radiates from joy in your heart.

I don't know of a more difficult profession on this planet than being a pastor. A pastor is somewhat like the president of the United States; his popularity index and approval rating is like an ocean wave—up one moment and down the next. I constantly have to choose to maintain my joy—even after complaints about the music, gripes about the temperature, or second-guessing one statement I may make out of a 40-minute message.

> People of influence choose joy over gloom,
> gladness over sadness, optimism over pessimism—
> and lead others to do the same thing.

When I find myself tempted to chuck it all in and lose the smile in my heart, I remember Victor Frankl. He was a Nazi concentration camp survivor. He describes how everything tangible was taken from the Jewish prisoners—clothing, personal belongings, pictures. In the ultimate dignity robbing degradation, their captors even removed their names and gave them numbers. I ask you—where do you find joy in *that* situation? But then Frankl says: "Everything can be taken from a man but one thing: the last of human freedoms—to choose one's attitude in any given set of circumstances."[1]

People of influence choose joy over gloom, gladness over sadness, optimism over pessimism—and lead others to do the same thing. Life is indeed short, and the journey is over almost from the time it begins. Beginning today, make it a joy ride!

Principle Two—*Joy:* By your words and deeds, let the joy of a loving God shine through your life to others.

Chapter Three

In the Eye of the Storm

*"First keep the peace within yourself then
you can also bring peace to others."*

THOMAS À KEMPIS, 1420

I n a recent interview, Barbara Walters asked highly accomplished actor Richard Dreyfuss a probing question: "If you could have one wish, what would you wish for?" Without hesitating, Dreyfuss replied, "Every time I have a birthday, every time I blow out candles, every time I see a shooting star, I wish the same thing—I wish for inner security." In other words, he wished for peace. I have a feeling that Dreyfuss is like many people today who long for personal peace.

What do men want most in their homes? A survey taken a few years ago revealed a surprising answer to what men care most about and hope their wives understand. Men did not want expensive furniture, well-equipped garages, or a private study. What they wanted most was tranquility at home. In other words, they wanted peace.

While in Israel, I once took a taxi down to the old city of Jerusalem. The young Jewish cab driver, Asi, responded eagerly to my questions about spiritual matters.

"What do you believe about the Messiah?" I asked.

"I believe the most important thing that can ever happen to Israel is for the Messiah to come," he said.

"Why do you believe that?"

"Because He will bring peace!"

We all long for peace—whether personal peace or political peace. We want peace with our next-door neighbors and between nations as well. In more than 3500 years of recorded civilization, only 286 years have been spent without war raging someplace on the globe. Yet during that same period, 8000 peace treaties have been signed. Someone pungently observed, "Peace is the brief, glorious moment in history when everybody stands around reloading."

> The primary cause of our difficulty in maintaining external peace is our lack of internal peace.

Do you realize that all of the peace monuments in Washington DC were built after a war? I am convinced that the primary cause of our difficulty in maintaining external peace is our lack of internal peace. Recently, I saw a large plaque near the United Nations building in New York City bearing Isaiah 2:4:

> They will beat their swords into plowshares,
>   and their spears into pruning hooks.
> Nation will not take up sword against nation,
>   nor will they train for war anymore.

Unfortunately, this prophecy is yet to be fulfilled, as the news reminds us daily.

Even though part of the UN charter reads, "Our purpose is to maintain international peace and security and to that end:

to take effective, collective measures for the prevention and removal of threats to the peace," I am convinced that this noble goal is doomed without peace of another sort. The kind of peace I want to address is more than the absence of war; it is the presence of an inward, personal peace that doesn't depend on the ever-changing circumstances of life and cannot be blown about by the winds of current events. I mean the inner confidence that God is in control of all circumstances, which allows one to face every difficulty with faith not fear.

Most of us long for that kind of peace, and it is a crucial step to becoming a person of influence and impact.

It's Tough Out There

We live in the most technologically advanced time in history. My life and my job are radically different today than they were even 10 years ago, and I'm grateful for the many amenities that make my life easier. I would be dead in the water were it not for cell phones, fax machines, email, laptops, the Internet, laser printers, photocopy machines, jet planes, and automobiles equipped with global positioning systems.

Yet these technological marvels create their own problems. A *USA Today* article detailed how high-tech gadgets boost not only productivity but stress. It described how therapist Ofér Zur staged a conference called "Speed.com: The Search for Meaning in the New Millennium" in the heart of stressed-out Silicon Valley. Zur could see the drawn faces, worried looks, and preoccupied demeanors in his audience. He said "his personal alarm sounded when patients started bringing cell phones and laptops to his practice—and using them during the session!"

Zur further observed, "We've become obsessed with speed. We end up with lots of plans that we can't execute and a full schedule that can't be followed. The paradox of our timesaving tech gadgets is that we've wound up with no free time."

One stressed-out secretary told her boss, "When this rush is over, I'm going to have a nervous breakdown. I earned it. I deserve it. And nobody's going to take it from me!" Can you relate to this woman? Frankly, at this stage of my life I am so busy that I don't have the time to have a nervous breakdown—and if I did, I would be too busy to enjoy it!

Without question, our warp-speed pace has added to the mess of stress and is taking a heavy toll. In short, *increasing our pace has decreased our peace.* Not long ago we marked the passage of time in seasons. But seasons begat monthly calendars, which begat day planners, which begat one-minute managers, which begat handheld personal organizers.

> Our warp-speed pace has added to the mess of stress and is taking a heavy toll.

One can see cyber-stress and hyper-stress everywhere. Go to the grocery store and see how much small talk you get from the cashier, whose speed and efficiency is being tracked by computer even as she electronically scans your groceries, calls out your total, and digitally sweeps you out the door. Try engaging telephone solicitors or directory-assistance operators in any meaningful dialogue, and you won't succeed; they work under precise, by-the-minute efficiency guidelines. The result of this fast-paced, time-warped approach? Increasing impatience, intolerance, and a lack of civility.

The workplace is a major incubator where stress is fed, nurtured, and kept warm. Lou Harris and Associates conducted a national study of the changing workforce for the Families and

Work Institute. This five-year study sought in-depth information from nearly 3000 salaried and hourly employees. When asked a variety of questions about how tough today's jobs are, 88 percent of the respondents said they work "very hard"; 68 percent said they work "very fast"; 60 percent said they still don't get work done; 71 percent feel "used up." The research concluded, "Workers are more frazzled, insecure, and torn between work and family than they were in 1977."

Not even ministers are immune. I sometimes get depressed at the constant barrage of things that scream for my immediate attention. Emails multiply daily like rabbits. Turn off your cell phone even for a couple of hours, and when you turn it back on, it has gained 10 pounds just from the added voicemails. And don't get me started on texting and tweeting!

I can relate to a *Los Angeles Times* article in which psychologist Richard Blackmon claimed, "Pastors are the single most occupationally frustrated group in America." About 75 percent of pastors go through a period of stress so great that they consider quitting the ministry; 35 to 40 percent actually resign. Incidents of mental breakdown are so high that insurance companies charge about 4 percent extra to cover church staff members, compared to employees in other professions.

> No one is immune to stress, frustration, and the feeling that we are on the autobahn of life.

H.B. London of Focus on the Family cites a Fuller Institute of Church Growth study that found 90 percent of pastors work more than 46 hours a week; 90 percent believe they have inadequate training to cope with ministry demands; 50 percent feel unable to meet the needs of the job; 75 percent report a significant stress-related crisis at least once in their ministry; 80 percent believe that pastoral ministry has a negative effect on their families; and 33 percent say that being in the ministry is downright hazardous to their families.

I am not whining or complaining. I'm just telling you I live in the same zip code of life that you do. I experience stress, occupational demands, deadlines, and personal pressures ganging up on me and constantly trying to rob me of the peace we all desperately desire.

No one is immune to stress, frustration, and the feeling that we are on the autobahn of life. What is all this but the absence of peace. In this maelstrom of daily living, the stock value of peace increases every moment.

Making Peace

Did you know a manual exists that holds the secret to peace? I mean *real* peace, not the artificial peace that people look for in a pill, a bottle, or a transient experience. The Bible speaks a great deal about peace, describing three kinds in particular.

First, you can attain peace *with others*. "If it is possible, as far as it depends on you, live at peace with everyone," said the apostle Paul in Romans 12:18. This is *external* peace, necessary for human relationships to flourish, whether in neighborhoods or nations.

Second, you can achieve peace *with yourself*. The Scripture speaks of letting the "peace of Christ rule in your hearts" (Colossians 3:15). This is *internal* peace, the inner tranquility that escapes most people today.

Finally, the Bible speaks of peace *with God*. "Therefore, since we have been justified through faith, we have peace with God through our Lord Jesus Christ" (Romans 5:1). This is *eternal* peace. It comes from knowing that one has a right relationship with the sovereign God of this universe.

Peace Is a Process

How many times have you heard the words *peace process* concerning the strife in the Middle East? Even though the process doesn't seem to be working, the concept is right—peace is a process. Peace is not a goal to be achieved but a process where one type of peace achieved leads to another. You cannot be at true peace with others until you are at peace with yourself. But you can never be truly at peace with yourself unless you are at peace with God, for all true peace flows from the only One who can give peace.

> People are looking for peace today in every place but the right place.

People are looking for peace today in every place but the right place. Why? Because they do not understand where true peace comes from. Some try to find peace in pills or pleasure or possessions, but they discover too late that these things offer only a synthetic, counterfeit peace that always wears off and wears out.

In 1987, Minnesota Twins superstar Kirby Puckett saw a childhood dream come true when he led his team to a World Series championship. Greg Gagne, the Twins shortstop, was asked to describe the scene in the clubhouse after their win. He recounted the hugging, the shouting, the laughing, the obligatory dousing of champagne over the players' heads, and the presentation of the trophy. But the memory that would stick with him forever, he said, occurred when he noticed the normally ebullient Puckett sitting silently on a stool away from everyone, only 10 minutes into the celebration. Gagne wove his way through the media, players, and coaches, sat down beside Puckett, and asked him to describe his thoughts. With a deep sadness in his eyes, Puckett said, "If this is all there is to it, life is pretty empty."

You may be able to relate to that ballplayer. You may have a great job, an excellent salary, a fine house, a wonderful family, good health, and maybe even a low golf handicap—but *no real personal peace.* You lack the inward peace that assures you that even though life often feels like a runaway roller coaster, Someone has a hand on the throttle keeping everything under control.

The Hebrew term for this kind of peace is *shalom.* Apart from God, enduring peace will always remain a pipe dream, a philosophical fantasy, a tantalizing fish always just beyond any bait or hook.

Where Peace Can Always Be Found

Let me let you in on a secret. Peace is not the absence of problems but the presence of God in the midst of your problems. Most people never find peace because they are looking for it. No one ever finds peace by looking for peace. Peace is not something you find; it finds you when you focus on the God who gives peace.

> Peace is not the absence of problems but the presence of God in the midst of your problems.

Many marriages go awry because men and women think an imperfect person can give them the perfect peace they are searching for. Have you heard the story of a woman at a cocktail party trying her best to look happy? Someone noticed a gargantuan sparkling rock on her finger and exclaimed, "Wow! What a beautiful diamond!"

"Yes," she said, "it's a Callahan diamond."

"I wish I had one!" the onlooker replied.

"No, you don't," the woman said.

"Why not?"

"Because it comes with the Callahan curse."

"The Callahan curse—what's that?"

She sighed and said, "Mr. Callahan!"

Perfect peace can come only from a perfect peace-giver, and the only One who meets that qualification is God!

People are looking not only for peace but also for those who manifest that peace in their lives. The great leaders who inspire great followings project a sense of serenity and peace even when everything around them is falling apart. The peers of Abraham Lincoln commented that even in the darkest days of the Civil War, when the North endured defeat after defeat, the president never displayed a sense of panic in his heart or on his face. Instead, he manifested a peace born of an unshakable confidence in a provident God and a just cause.

> The great leaders who inspire great followings project a sense of serenity and peace even when everything around them is falling apart.

Lincoln knew what a lot of stressed-out worrywarts need to learn: *Peace is a matter of focus.* A tremendous passage of Scripture states,

> You keep him in perfect peace
>> whose mind is stayed on you,
> because he trusts in you.
>> (Isaiah 26:3 ESV)

Focusing on circumstances will cause anxiety, for circumstances constantly change and often spin beyond our control. But God never changes and nothing spins beyond His control.

Peace and worry are mutually exclusive. Worry throttles our confidence, chokes our perspective, and suffocates our spirit. Worry robs us of the peace that comes from knowing the God who can handle anything and for whom all things are possible. The reason we worry is that we do exactly the opposite of the actions that bring peace.

Worry is a "vote of no confidence" in God. Every time you worry, you are really saying, "God, I don't believe You can handle this. I don't believe You can be trusted in this matter. I guess I'm going to have to carry this burden all by myself."

> Worry is a "vote of no confidence" in God.

When you worry, you are really saying that God does not keep His promises. You think He lies or exaggerates when He says things such as the promise of Romans 8:28: "And we know that in all things God works for the good of those who love him, who have been called according to his purpose."

I wish we could all take a cue from a man who was a tremendous worrier. He not only worried; he worried others with his worry. He couldn't sleep because he worried so much. All he would do was pace the floor. One day he came out of his house a totally different person. He was whistling and singing at the top of his lungs. His next-door neighbor saw him and asked, "What in the world has happened to you?"

"Oh," he replied, "I don't have a worry in this world, and I am so happy."

"And how did you get rid of your worries?" the neighbor asked.

"Well, I have hired a professional worrier. He does all my worrying for me."

"That's just wonderful. How much does this professional worrier cost?"

"He costs a thousand dollars a day."

"A thousand dollars a day? You don't have that kind of money. How are you going to pay him?"

"Oh, that's his worry," the man said.

You can give *all* your problems to Someone so you can enjoy peace even in the most difficult times. If you follow just one Scripture verse, it will bring peace in every situation: "Cast all your anxiety on him because he cares for you" (1 Peter 5:7).

No Need to Panic

One of the most powerful natural forces known to man is a hurricane. With winds of up to 155 miles per hour, rain up to 5 inches per hour, and the ability to create waves 10 stories high and wave surges up to 25 feet wide, hurricanes can level whole cities in minutes. Two components of a hurricane are especially interesting. One is the eye of a hurricane—the relatively calm center in which sinking air inhibits cloud and thunderstorm development. Immediately surrounding the eye is the eyewall, which features rising air and powerful rain clouds. In sharp contrast to the calm eye, the eyewall houses the most powerful element of the hurricane, including the strongest winds and the heaviest rains.

If you could hover above this incredibly powerful force of nature, you would see the strongest part of a hurricane occurring near its center, while at its center is relative calm, with no thunderstorms and little or no cloud cover.

Many years ago I was thrust, through no real fault of my own, into a great crisis in my ministry. It's one of the most painful episodes of my life. Even recounting this event causes my stomach to knot up and feelings of fear to wash over me. Through the incompetence and irresponsibility of a trusted associate, I woke up one morning to discover that our church was in deep financial trouble—broke, 90 to 120 days in arrears on hundreds of thousands of dollars of unpaid bills. Conveniently, the person primarily responsible had moved on to another organization and left me holding the proverbial bag. (Not so coincidentally, the organization he went to experienced financial troubles leading to his and others' terminations.)

I still remember walking into a meeting with the seven shell-shocked people who served on our finance team. They had also just learned of our dire situation and were giving me that "what are you going to do to get us out of this mess" look. I knew then that I was facing one of the greatest tests of organizational leadership in my life. My reaction would determine whether we would weather the storm. Either they would see panic in my eyes or sense a peace in my heart.

The meeting was the shortest of my career. I said one thing: "Gentlemen, I didn't get us into this mess, but with God's help we *will* get out of it." I closed the meeting with prayer and left. I didn't tell them I didn't have a clue what I was going to do. I wish I could tell you that I didn't weep, worry, and wring my hands as I wrestled with this situation. But what kept me calm in the eye of this storm was the unwavering conviction that God was in control. I was confident that if I would trust Him to do His part and I did mine, I could accept the consequences of my actions and the results of His.

> People are drawn to those who can keep their
> head when everyone else is losing theirs.

I am thankful that we did get through this and even came out stronger as a church because of it. But the great lesson I learned is that people are drawn to those who can keep their head when everyone else is losing theirs.

Oceanographers tell us that the worst ocean storm never goes more than 25 feet beneath the surface. Gales can rip the ocean, causing tidal waves 100 feet high. But just 25 feet below the surface, the water is as calm as a pond on a sunny day in June.

The only place you will ever find peace in the midst of the storm is down deep in a walk with God. The peace found in God, through the Holy Scriptures and prayer, cannot be found, bought, or manufactured anywhere else. The Korean Christians have a saying that emerged from the persecution they have endured because of their faith in Christ. "We are just like nails," they say. "The harder you hit us, the deeper you drive us; and the deeper you drive us, the more peaceful it becomes."

Part of God's purpose in allowing the storms to blow is to drive us deeper. Deeper into dependence, deeper into relationship with Him. Someone once said, "God takes life's broken pieces and gives us unbroken peace." When you focus on the One who has never met a problem He can't solve instead of focusing on the problem you can't solve, you will become a person of peace who exercises incredible influence over others.

People are drawn to peaceful leaders; they are inspired by those who have inner stillness and calm. Think of George Washington at Valley Forge, Franklin Roosevelt proclaiming "we have nothing to fear but fear itself," or Ronald Reagan pushing the country through turmoil to a "shining city on a hill."

Become a person of peace, and others will seek your advice when they face trouble. Furthermore, they will join forces with you when you are *all* in trouble. If the God within you reigns above you, you will not succumb to what is around you. Seek peace and become influential beyond your imagination.

Principle Three — *Peace:* Respond to every difficult situation believing that God will lead you through it and that His peace will build confidence in your ability to influence others.

Chapter Four

A Snail's Pace Can Be Fast Enough

*"Patience and perseverance have a magical effect before
which difficulties disappear and obstacles vanish."*

JOHN QUINCY ADAMS

A first-grade teacher and her class of 32 pupils watched it rain all day. Finally, the last bell rang signaling time to go home, and the teacher began putting galoshes on all her students. She came to the last girl relieved that her dirty task was almost finished. Yet the galoshes seemed unusually tight. The teacher struggled, she strained, she pulled, she tugged, she grunted, she groaned—and finally got the galoshes on. Just as she finished snapping them into place, the girl said, "You know what, teacher? These aren't my galoshes."

The teacher couldn't believe it. With a tremendous sigh she struggled, she strained, she pulled, she tugged, she grunted, she groaned, until glistening with sweat she finally yanked the galoshes off the girl's feet. At the moment she snapped them off, the little girl looked up at her and said sweetly, "They're my sister's, and she lets me wear them."

Ah, patience. This is the one virtue I hate waiting on. I am notoriously impatient. I often tell God, "I want patience, and I want it right now!" Lack of patience is my emotional Achilles' heel. When I meet someone who is patient, I often come to admire them.

I need to be more like the little boy in a department store. He was at the end of an escalator, watching the railing as it went around. A salesman came by and asked him, "Son, are you lost?"

"No," the little boy said, "I'm just waiting for my chewing gum to come back."

Little in life has ever been accomplished without the virtue of patience.

Another word for patience is *long-suffering*, which describes this character trait well. Long-suffering is more than suffering for a long time, which is what patience feels like at times. Long-suffering is the willingness to exercise patience, perseverance, and persistence in the pursuit of worthy goals. It's the ability to be slow to anger, slow to lose hope, and slow to quit even when everyone around you is acting with impatience.

> Long-suffering is the willingness to exercise patience, perseverance, and persistence in the pursuit of worthy goals.

Some situations can be successfully handled only by "going at a snail's pace." That's why patience and perseverance are twin towers of strength to leaders who make maximum impact and have positive influence on the lives of others.

If you are going to be a person of influence, there are three principles about patience that you must never forget.

Difficult People Must Be Handled with Patience

Years ago a man decided to join a monastery because he was tired of dealing with difficult people. He rose to become the head monk and felt deliriously happy. Then a new man joined the community, and the head monk told the man the rule everybody had to keep: *Say only two words every year.*

At the end of the first year the head monk asked the man, "What are your two words?"

"Bed hard," the man said.

At the end of the second year the man once again trudged into the head monk's office.

"What are your two words for this year?" the head monk asked.

"Room cold," he said with a glare.

The head monk fought back a retort, but instead bowed his head and sent the man away.

At the end of the third year, the man entered with balled fists and trembling lips.

"What are your two words for this year?" the head monk reluctantly asked.

"Food terrible," the man said.

The head monk didn't say a word, but his look could kill.

Finally, at the end of the fourth year, the man walked in and screamed, "I quit!"

"That's just great!" the head monk shot back. "All you've done since you've been here is complain, complain, complain!"

Nobody can avoid dealing with difficult people. Not even monks in monasteries are exempt. If you are a person of influence, you need to learn how to deal patiently with difficult people.

One can learn much about patience by observing ordinary farmers. Farmers plant, pull weeds, cultivate, and harvest. Every day before the harvest, a farmer will do at least two things: watch and wait. He knows that the harvest will come if he will just be patient. So he watches for problems that need solving while he waits for his precious crops to grow. A farmer knows that he cannot hurry the harvest. It will come in due time.

What is true of farmers is also true of you as a leader. It takes supernatural patience to wait for the harvest. Anyone can explode when people blow it. It takes a special person to respond with grace and calmness when the heat is on because somebody else started the fire.

Of course, patience is not passivity or indifference. It is not a fatalistic attitude toward life that sits back, twiddles its thumbs, and says, "Whatever will be, will be." Patience does not mean that you never get angry; anger is not always wrong. Sometimes a lack of anger is wrong.

Patience means you are slow to anger and quick to get rid of it. Too often we are just the opposite: We are quick to be angry and slow to get rid of it—and that is when the acid of anger turns into the burden of bitterness. Then we either hold grudges or try to get even. We can even appear to be patient with others when we really are not. A friend used to say to me, "Patience is the ability to idle your motor when you feel like stripping your gears." I like that metaphor.

> "Patience is the ability to idle your motor when you feel like stripping your gears."

Some American soldiers during the Korean War rented a house and hired a local boy to do their housekeeping and cooking. Their little Korean fellow had an unbelievably positive attitude—he was always smiling and jovial, and they especially loved his broken English. They played one trick after another on him. They nailed his shoes to the floor. He would just get up in the morning, pull out the nails with pliers, and keep on smiling. They put grease on the stove handles. He would just wipe off the handles and keep smiling and singing. They balanced buckets of water over the door so that when he opened the door, he would get drenched. He would dry off and never fuss and keep on smiling.

Finally, they became so ashamed of themselves that they called him in and said, "We want you to know that we are never going to trick you again. We really do appreciate your patience."

"You mean, no more nail shoes to floor?" he asked.

"No more."

"You mean, no more sticky on stove knobs?"

"No more."

"You mean, no more water buckets on door?"

"No more."

"OK then," he said, "no more spit in soup."

Many of us have seen the bumper sticker that states: "Please be patient with me; God is not finished with me yet." I'm glad God is patient with me, but to be a person of influence, I need to infuse my life with patience.

> The people you love the most will try your patience the most.

You cannot get away from people who are going to try your patience. In fact, the people you love the most will try your patience the most. Think about marriage. By and large, marriages fail for one basic reason: One or both spouses simply quit. In any relationship, whether at home or at the office, patience can salvage partnerships that are really worth keeping.

Difficulties are opportunities in disguise to help you cultivate the virtue of patience.

People are attracted to leaders who display patience. They will navigate toward those who possess the ability to control their emotions during the most trying of circumstances. I think about my closest advisors through the years—John, Brad, Mark, Larry, Bruce, Bob. I think of some of my best friends—Danny, Scott, Pick, Ken, Buddy, Chris. In each person, I find incredible patience. The reason I confide in them and have grown close to them is that their patient spirit gives them emotional stability. And when I surround myself with stable advisors, I become confident in my decisions.

Demanding Problems Must Be Handled with Perseverance

Perseverance is a first cousin to patience. As I look back on life, I can see that my meaningful accomplishments did not come without difficulties and opposition. Along the way, I always had the option to give up, give out, or give in—but only if I wanted to admit defeat.

One of my heroes is a man we hear little about, but he affects the lives of millions around the world who turn on a light or listen to recorded music. His influence lives on today because he maintained an unswerving, even steely determination to see projects through to completion. The Recording Academy, known for its GRAMMY awards, honored this man with its Technical GRAMMY Award for 2010. He had an astounding number of inventions—1093—and held more patents than any other person in the world, receiving at least one every year for 65 consecutive years. He also developed the modern research laboratory. My hero's name is Thomas Alva Edison.

Edison and his catalog of inventions have been profoundly influential. Most experts credit his creative genius, but he credited his success to hard work. "Genius," he declared, "is 99 percent perspiration and 1 percent inspiration." He succeeded, in part, because of his positive attitude. The optimistic Edison saw the best in everything. "If we did all the things we were capable of doing," he once said, "we would literally astound ourselves."

After 10,000 tries, he still couldn't find the right material for the incandescent lightbulb, but he didn't see the unsuccessful attempts as failures. With each attempt he gained information about what didn't work, bringing him closer to a solution. He never doubted that he would find a good one. His belief could be summarized by this statement: "Many of life's failures are people who did not realize how close they were to success when they gave up."

Every time I turn on a light, I am so grateful that Edison didn't quit. His perseverance has given light to billions.

Here's the bad news: Everybody has problems. But have you ever considered why? God could have put us in a problem-free world (actually He did, but we blew it). Unfortunately, we live in a world that is chock-full of problems on all seven continents.

> Problems are not tools to tear you
> down but tests to build you up.

Here's the good news: Problems are not meant to defeat you, depress you, or discourage you. God meant them to develop you. Problems are not tools to tear you down but tests to build you up. One mark of a successful person is the ability to see problems as opportunities rather than obstacles. The greatest lessons you will ever learn occur not when you party during the good times but when you persevere in the bad times. Indeed, that is why the bad times make the good times so good.

Have you ever read about the birth of a giraffe? The first parts to emerge are the baby's front hooves and head. Then the entire calf appears and tumbles 10 feet to the ground, landing on its back. Within seconds it rolls over and stands, struggling with those gangly, untried legs. Then an amazing thing happens: The mother giraffe positions herself directly over her newborn calf and looks it over. Then she swings a long leg outward and kicks that baby, sending it sprawling. If it doesn't get up, she kicks it again. If it grows tired, she kicks it again to stimulate its efforts to stand.

Each time the baby giraffe manages to get to its feet, its mother kicks it over again. The mother's actions may seem cruel to us, but she is preparing that little calf for survival. The calf must learn to get up quickly and run with the herd when danger comes, or it will not survive.

When life knocks you down, you have to get back up. At certain times, you may even have to stand or die—some situations leave no other choice. During those difficult times, you will learn some of the greatest lessons through sheer determination and perseverance.

William Wilberforce was a member of the British Parliament and a dear friend of John Newton, the former slave owner who wrote the beloved hymn, "Amazing Grace." Wilberforce was a tremendous Christian who crusaded in Parliament to outlaw slavery throughout the British Empire. He begged, pleaded, and introduced bills, and each time he would be laughed down, shouted down, and voted down. When he was on his deathbed, the British Parliament finally signed the bill outlawing slavery. How long did it take? Fifty years. Thank God he didn't quit.

Don't Quit

When things go wrong, as they sometimes will,
When the road you're trudging seems all uphill,
When the funds are low and the debts are high,
And you want to smile, but you have to sigh,
When care is pressing you down a bit...
Rest if you must, but don't you dare quit.
When you are worried and full of doubt,
Just remember that success is failure turned inside out...
So stick to the fight when you're hardest hit,
It's when things seem worst that you mustn't quit.

AUTHOR UNKNOWN

No one can guarantee that perseverance will bring success. But it is certain that if you lack perseverance—if you leave the kitchen every time things heat up—you are headed for failure. You are not a failure until you quit, but when you quit, you fail. As the old saying goes, quitters never win and winners never quit.

You are not a failure until you quit, but when you quit, you fail.

I want to let you in on a little secret: Failure is not necessarily a bad thing. Failure—and how you respond to it—truly reveals your inner strength, your force of will, and the character of your soul.

Let's try a little exercise. Write on a piece of paper the one feat you would accomplish in life if you could pick only one thing. Then attach that paper to your mirror or computer monitor or place it somewhere you'll see it every day. For 30 days do two things: (1) Every time you see it, say to yourself, *Just for today, I'm going to take one step toward achieving this goal,* and (2) take that one step. Patiently persevere for 30 days uninterrupted. At the end of that month, you will be amazed at how much of that weight you lost, how much of that book you read, how much of that money you were able to save. And to boot, you will have seen the awesome power of determination.

Dynamic Purposes Are Fulfilled with Persistence

You can unlock impact and influence by exercising patience and perseverance, but you should also develop the discipline of persistence. These three traits go hand in hand, and they'll help shape those around you (not to mention yourself).

These traits are difficult to develop because they involve waiting, and we don't like that. It's one of the more difficult things we have to do in life. In a country that survives on frozen dinners, instant mashed potatoes, packaged cake mixes, wireless Internet, and freeway express lanes, it's difficult to wait. If the truth were known, sometimes we would rather do the wrong thing than wait.

Good leaders know how to wait. They know that the most successful leaders are persistent leaders. Troubles and troublemakers come into your life to force you to "suffer long," but you will never reach the peak of your potential until you learn the discipline of persistence.

JELL-O celebrated its one-hundredth anniversary in 1997. However, if its inventor were still alive, he probably would have taken little comfort in his product's success. In 1897, Pearl Wait wore several hats. He was a construction worker who also dabbled in patent medicines and went door-to-door selling his remedies.

In the midst of his tinkering, he came upon the idea of mixing fruit flavoring with granulated gelatin. His wife named it JELL-O, and Wait thought he had one more product to peddle.

Unfortunately, initial sales of his jiggly snack were not as strong as he had hoped, so Pearl Wait hastily sold his JELL-O rights to Orator Woodward for $450. Woodward knew the value of marketing, and within eight brief years, he turned a $450 investment into a $1 million business. Today, not a single relative of Pearl Wait receives one penny from the 1.1 million boxes of JELL-O sold every day. Why not? Because Wait just couldn't wait.

Instant success is a myth, whether with people or problems. If one needs to lose ten pounds or a hundred, the weight can be shed only one pound at a time. Standing on top of the mountain is a thrill, but getting there through a determined climb makes it all worthwhile. Almost every significant success came at the end of a long wait.

Instant success is a myth.

Though I grew up in Georgia and love my home state, when it comes to baseball, I am unashamedly a New York Yankees fan. I grew up listening to Dizzy Dean and Pee Wee Reese call Major League Baseball's *Game of the Week* every Saturday afternoon, which often featured the Yankees. My hero and idol was Mickey Mantle.

One of my greatest thrills was the time I went with my son Jonathan to see the Yankees play the Atlanta Braves at historic Yankee Stadium. This was hallowed ground for a Yankees fan, and I almost lost control when I saw the monuments in centerfield to Babe Ruth, Lou Gehrig, and Joe DiMaggio. Does it get any better?

At the time, the Yankees had won four of the last six World Series and three in a row from 1998 to 2000. By all accounts, the team's success was due in no small part to the leadership of their manager, Joe Torre. His face was plastered all over magazines and featured in many commercials.

What many do not know is that it took Joe Torre 4272 games as a player and a manager to get to the World Series—the longest wait for anyone in the history of the game. Torre reflected on his achievements, so long in the making:

> As a manager prior to coming to the Yankees, my win-loss record was 119 games below .500…[yet] I never gave in to the idea that I was somehow a failure… Baseball is such a perfect metaphor for life [because its] 162-game schedule—the "grind" I have known for thirty-two years—is in fact much closer to the daily lives of most people. You get up every morning, do your best, make small steps forward, suffer setbacks that obscure your long-term progress, fight off hassles and absurd obstacles, and once in a blue moon, you actually achieve a cherished goal that's been the stuff of your dreams. Then, with the world's permission, you can call yourself a winner. But only you know how many small triumphs and snarls went into that big victory, how many months, years, or decades of sweat and sorrow preceded that breakthrough. That's baseball, and that's life.

Joe Torre is living proof that if you quit, you never win, nor will you live in the truest sense of the word. He waited a long time to achieve success, and he is still revered as one of the best managers in all of baseball. Torre's career teaches us an invaluable lesson. Those who determine to fight until their last breath will always end up winners.

> **Principle Four—** *Patience:* Just for today, in dealing with people and problems, hang in there and don't quit!

Chapter Five

You Can't Be Too Kind

"Commit a random act of kindness."
BILLBOARD MESSAGE OUTSIDE OF HIGHLANDS, NC

After Confederate general Robert E. Lee retired from the military, he was named president of Washington and Lee University in Lexington, Virginia. Washington and Lee was originally named Washington Academy because of a gift from George Washington, but the name was changed in 1871 in honor of Robert E. Lee.

While Lee served as president of the university, a new student came into his office and asked for a copy of the school's rules and regulations. Lee looked at him and said, "Son, we don't have any rules and regulations in print."

"You mean, this school has no rules?" the young man asked.

"We have only one," Lee said.

"What is it?"

"Our only rule is kindness."

Whatever Happened to Kindness?

We live in a society in which kindness is becoming an increasingly rare commodity. Not long ago, the cover story of *USA Today* began with this observation: "A surly driver cuts into your lane. Your teenager brings home a CD with lewd, hostile lyrics.

A political candidate in a TV ad morphs into a convicted murderer. A star baseball player spits at an umpire. A radio talk show jockey insults the president while he's sitting right there...it is impossible to ignore the growing rudeness, even harshness, of American life."

Shortly after this in 2005, British writer Lynne Truss wrote the widely sold book, *Talk to the Hand: The Utter Bloody Rudeness of the World Today, or Six Good Reasons to Stay Home and Bolt the Door*. In it, she rants on the plummeting social standards of the twenty-first century. From traffic accidents to massive telephone hold times, we've become accustomed to treating each other poorly.

As recently as 2009, my friend Mark DeMoss launched a movement known as The Civility Project. He was moved by the religion-based attacks on Mitt Romney during his run for the presidency. A known conservative, DeMoss was impressed by the genteel spirit displayed by Hillary Clinton ally and advisor Lanny Davis during the campaign. DeMoss reached out to him, and Davis decided to join in the effort to restore civility in public life. The project is built around taking the civility pledge: "I will be civil in my public discourse and behavior. I will be respectful of others whether or not I agree with them. I will stand against incivility when I see it."

> In the glass of our current society, it seems
> the milk of human kindness has curdled.

I am convinced that DeMoss's project could not have been birthed a moment too soon. An overwhelming majority of Americans—89 percent in a *U.S. News and World Report* poll—think incivility is a serious problem. More than three in four respondents said it has gotten worse in the last 10 years. In the glass of our current society, it seems the milk of human kindness has curdled.

When we see people as numbers or inconveniences rather than as individuals, kindness goes out the window. This is precisely what humorist Robert Henry encountered one evening when he visited a large discount department store in search of a pair of binoculars. As he walked up to the appropriate counter, he noticed he was the only customer in the store. Behind the counter stood two salespeople. One was so preoccupied talking to "Mama" on the telephone that she refused even to acknowledge Robert. At the other end of the counter, a second salesperson was unloading inventory from a box onto the shelves. Growing impatient, Robert walked down to her end of the counter and just stood there. Finally, she looked up at Robert and said, "You got a number?"

"I got a *what?*" asked Robert, trying to control his astonishment.

"You got a number? You gotta have a number."

"Lady, I'm the only customer in the store! I don't need a number. Can't you see how ridiculous this is?"

She insisted that Robert take a number before agreeing to wait on him. Robert went to the number dispenser, pulled number 37, and walked back to the salesperson. With that, she promptly went to her number counter, which revealed that the last customer had been holding number 34. She screamed out, "Number 35...35...36...36...37!"

"I'm number 37," Robert said.

"May I help you?" she asked without cracking a smile.

"No," Robert said, and he turned around and walked out.

I surfed the Internet recently looking for the word *kindness* and discovered a nonprofit organization called "The Kindness Society." Note their stated purpose: "We are striving to spread kindness by following a simple rule: Do not think, speak, or act unkindly toward others." Everybody can relate to kindness and everyone can respond with kindness. Mark Twain once said, "Kindness is a language which the deaf can hear, and the blind can read." Kindness is also the language that influential people speak.

Kindness is the effort to talk to people respectfully, to treat people graciously, and to take every opportunity to serve others sacrificially whenever possible. On the surface, one would think that would be easy to do, but it isn't. Being kind can be risky and even downright difficult. Kindness is risky because it can be misunderstood. We have all endured those experiences where we tried to be kind, but our efforts were taken the wrong way or we unwittingly said the wrong thing.

A woman carried her newborn onto a bus, and the driver said, "That's the ugliest baby I've ever seen!"

The lady slammed her money into the fare box and stomped back to a seat at the rear of the bus. The man next to her asked her what was wrong, and she said, "The bus driver was very rude to me!"

"That's outrageous," he said. "He shouldn't be insulting the passengers."

"I think I'll go up there and give him a piece of my mind," the lady said.

"Good idea. And while you're up there, I'll hold your monkey."

Sometimes kindness is the last thing on your mind. Sometimes giving the gift of kindness hurts. I think of the times I have passed broken-down cars on the highway and didn't even offer a phone call for help. I have allowed my business and the pressures of work to make me curt and short, knowing the moment I did so I had blown it.

I wish at such times I could be as quick thinking as a young man who worked in the produce section of a supermarket. A lady approached him on his first day on the job, requesting to buy half a head of lettuce. He tried to dissuade her, but she persisted. Finally he said, "I'll have to go back and talk to the manager."

He walked to the rear of the store, not realizing the woman had followed him. When he reached the manager, he said, "There's some stupid old lady out here who wants to buy half a head of lettuce. What should I tell her?"

Noting the horrified look on the manager's face, the boy turned around, saw the woman, and said, "And this nice lady wants to buy the other half."

> You can never be too kind. We all hunger to
> be treated with courtesy and kindness.

Sometimes when we pay people a compliment, they will coyly say, "You're too kind." What they're really screaming is, "Say it again!" You can never be too kind. We all hunger to be treated with courtesy and kindness.

People from all walks of life were attracted to Jesus for this reason. Jesus Christ would probably be universally acclaimed as the kindest person who ever lived. He, too, came into an unkind world, a dog-eat-dog, every-man-for-himself culture. No mental institutions, hospitals, orphanages, or organizations of mercy existed then. Yet when Jesus came, He poured the milk of human kindness into every bowl of human suffering. No one ever accused Him of being unkind, even His most bitter enemies.

He teaches us that we should be kind not only to those who don't deserve our kindness but also to those who are unappreciative. Even in His life, acts of kindness were misunderstood. His greatest act of kindness—His death on the cross—has been misunderstood and even reviled by much of the world. But He teaches us a real lesson about kindness: Kindness costs. Kindness costs a great deal, but it cannot be bought at any price.

Kindness Pays—BIG

Sometimes we think that influencers must be tough, hard, and stoic in the way they relate to others, so much so that kindness is viewed as a weakness or vulnerability for them. I strongly disagree. Kindness signals tremendous inner strength that others not only appreciate but respect.

> Tenderness and kindness can motivate people
> to do things that toughness never can.

Aesop wrote a fable in which the wind and the sun argued over who was the stronger.

"Do you see that old man down there?" the wind asked. "I can make him take his coat off quicker than you can."

The sun agreed to duck behind a cloud while the wind blew up a storm. As the wind blew, the man remained as he was. In fact, the harder the wind blew the more firmly the old man wrapped his coat around him.

Eventually, the wind gave up and the sun reappeared, smiling kindly upon that old man. Before long, the old man mopped his brow, pulled off his coat, and strolled on his way. The sun knew the secret: Warmth—friendliness and a gentle touch—is always stronger than force and fury.

In the same way, an influencer must learn how to motivate through warmth. One of the greatest marks of leadership—and one of the keys to building lasting relationships—is kindness. Being nice is important, but it is more important to be kind.

> Warmth—friendliness and a gentle touch—is
> always stronger than force and fury.

I think back to the teacher who motivated me to work harder as a student than any other teacher I ever had. Her name was Mrs. Propes, and she was my eighth-grade teacher. I was new to the school, shy, and timid around the bullies in the class. She went out of her way to encourage me, affirming me academically and making sure that I felt accepted—even protected at times! I was energized to do well in her class because I wanted to return her kindness with my best effort—not for the grades but for her approval.

This returns us to the topic of influence. Everyone knows that nothing leaves a more lasting influence than setting an example. The best and brightest leaders know that the best way to infuse an organization with a core value is to display that value in personal interaction.

Once while Abraham Lincoln was dining in the White House, one of his guests blew on his coffee, poured the coffee into his saucer, and drank out of the saucer. As you might imagine, some of the refined ladies seated near this guest were aghast. For a moment the room was filled with an embarrassing silence. Then Lincoln took his coffee, poured it into the saucer, and for the rest of the evening he also drank out of the saucer. Everyone else in the room followed suit. One small act of kindness had saved a man from unbelievable embarrassment. That simple yet thoughtful gesture by one of our greatest presidents reminds us of the value of setting an example of kindness. As William Wordsworth has said,

> That best portion of a good man's life;
> his little, nameless, unremembered acts of kindness
> and love.

You've probably never heard of Stephen Grellet, a French-born Quaker who died in New Jersey in 1855. He would remain unknown to the world today except for a few lines that will be remembered forever. "I shall pass through this world but once," he said. "Any good that I can do, or any kindness that I can show to any human being, let me do it now and not defer it. For I shall not pass this way again."

Every day has at least one thing in common with the next: the opportunity to show kindness. Let someone move in front of you in the flow of traffic. Open a door for a lady. Help people with their overhead luggage. Opportunities missed are not only gone but will leave you with unwanted regrets. I wish that everyone could remember this poem from an unknown author as opportunities arise to be kind.

> I have wept in the night
> For the shortness of sight
> That to somebody's need made me blind.
> But I never have yet
> Felt a twinge of regret
> For being a little too kind.

A Kind Word

Everyone has a "kindness kit" that they carry everywhere. It is called the tongue. Never underestimate the power of just one kind word. A Japanese proverb says, "One kind word can warm three winter months." It is easy to *react* to acts of kindness with kindness. The real challenge is to *respond* with kindness to those who lack it. Kindness flows easily to those who treat us well; it is difficult to be kind to those who don't. And we must be kind through our deeds and words.

> Never underestimate the power of just one kind word.

In the comic strip *Nancy,* Sluggo once said to Nancy, "That new kid in school is nothing but a big fathead!"

"You shouldn't call people names like that," Nancy said. "I never call people names."

"Well, I just got mad when he said you were stupid looking."

"What else did that big fathead say?" Nancy demanded.

Kindness is not softness. Kindness is not a sentimental indulgence that tolerates wrong and evil and refuses to confront a person when confrontation is required. Sometimes the kindest thing you can do is confront a person about a personal fault or problem.

Suppose my doctor discovers I have a tumor. He could say to himself, *I don't want to cause James any pain. I don't want to upset him in any way. I don't want him to leave here hurt or angry.* He brings me back into his office and says, "Everything looks great, James. Don't worry, be happy." That doctor is not being kind to me; he's being unkind. To be kind, that doctor must tell me the truth and try to remove that tumor, regardless of how much it may hurt.

Being kind does *not* mean being politically correct, tolerating wrongdoing, or refusing to confront a problem. Sometimes we must confront—yet in a kind way. A calm demeanor will go a lot farther than a harsh comment or an ugly tone of voice. You can make a critical point with a kind spirit, even a sense of humor.

A man was standing in line to buy an airline ticket. When he reached the counter, he said, "I would like to buy a ticket to New York City."

"No problem," the agent said. "How many pieces of luggage do you have?"

"I have three."

"Do you want to check all three to New York?"

"No, I want you to send the first suitcase to Phoenix, the second suitcase to Seattle, and the third suitcase to London."

The dumbfounded clerk looked at him and said, "Sir, I'm sorry, but we can't do that."

"I don't know why not," the man said with a smile. "That's what you did last week."

You can make your point with a butter knife more effectively than with a butcher knife.

Nice Guys Really Finish First

Aesop said, "No act of kindness, no matter how small, ever is wasted." It costs to be unkind, but it pays to be kind. Kindness always pays dividends, either for you or for someone else down the line. Kindness is never a waste of time or effort. It really is one link in an unbroken chain.

Joe was driving home one evening on a country road. Work

in this small Midwestern community was almost as slow as his beat-up Pontiac, but he never quit looking for a job. Ever since his factory had closed down, Joe had been unemployed. And with winter coming, he had reached a point of desperation.

It was dark, and Joe almost didn't see the old lady stranded on the side of the road. He pulled up in front of her Mercedes and got out. As he walked up to her, he sensed that she was frightened, standing out there alone in the cold.

"Ma'am, I'm just here to help you," Joe said. "Why don't you wait in the car where it's warm, and I'll see if I can repair your car. By the way, my name is Joe."

All she had was a flat tire, so Joe crawled under the car, looking for a place to put the jack. He scraped his hands on the hard rocks and stained his shirt with grease and dirt, but he was soon able to change the tire. As he was tightening the lug nuts, she rolled down her window and told him she was from St. Louis and was just passing through. She could not thank him enough for coming to her aid. He just smiled as he closed her trunk and started returning to his car.

"Tell me, how much do I owe you?" she asked. "I'll be glad to pay you anything you ask."

Joe looked back and said, "If you really want to pay me back, the next time you see someone who needs help, give them the help they need and then—just think of me."

He waited until she started her car and drove off.

That day had been cold and depressing, but Joe felt good as he headed home.

A few miles down the road, this same lady stopped at a small café to grab a bite to eat before she made the last leg of her trip home. It was a dingy-looking restaurant. One could tell business was not going well.

The waitress wore a sweet smile, and though she was pregnant and tired, she was eager to please. The woman could tell the waitress was struggling just to make ends meet. She wondered how someone with so little could cheerfully serve a stranger. Then she thought of Joe.

After the lady finished her meal, the waitress went to get her change from a $100 bill, but the lady was gone by the time the waitress returned. The waitress scanned the restaurant looking for her customer, but the only thing she found was a folded napkin on which the lady had written:

> You don't owe me a thing,
> I've been there too;
> Someone once helped me out
> The way I'm helping you.
> If you really want to pay me back,
> Here's what you do;
> Don't let the chain of kindness
> End with you.

The waitress's eyes welled up with tears of gratitude.

Later that night, when she got home from work and climbed into bed, she thought about the money and what the lady had written. *How could the woman have known how much my husband and I needed it?* With this baby coming next month, her shoestring budget was going to become fishing wire, especially with her husband out of work. She gave her slumbering husband a soft kiss and whispered, "Everything's going to be all right. I love you, Joe."

Ralph Waldo Emerson once said, "You cannot do a kindness too soon, for you never know how soon it will be too late." Take every opportunity to be kind.

The Kindness of God

One of my favorite passages of Scripture reminds us of the importance of kindness: "God raised us up with Christ and seated us with him in the heavenly realms in Christ Jesus, in order that in the coming ages he might show the incomparable riches of his grace, *expressed in his kindness to us* in Christ Jesus" (Ephesians 2:6-7). Kindness and eternity are incredibly linked. Don't miss it.

God sent Jesus Christ from heaven to earth so that we can leave earth and go to heaven. This is evidence of God's kindness, even to those who are not yet believers. Beyond that, the eternal presence of Christ will always remind us of God's great kindness for all eternity. God places so high a premium on kindness, He never wants us to forget it.

A Tale of Two Presidents

Kindness is one of the indispensable keys that unlock influence and impact. The power that flows from kind words, kind acts, or kind touches cannot be measured. Stories from two former U.S. presidents illustrate the incredible power in the lives of others that kindness can give.

> The power that flows from kind words, kind acts, or kind touches cannot be measured.

Kindness was a hallmark of President Ronald Reagan. Even the late president's political foes liked him and were often swayed by his charming kindness. Frances Green, an 83-year-old woman, lived by herself on Social Security in a rough neighborhood in Daly City, California. Though she was poor, she sent one dollar a year for eight years to the Republican National Committee.

One day she received an RNC fund-raising letter in the mail. The letter was cream-colored with black and gold writing, and it invited her to come to the White House to meet President Reagan. What she didn't notice was the little RSVP card. Neither did she notice the suggestion that if she were going to come, she should send in a generous donation. She thought she had been invited because they appreciated her yearly donation.

This lady rounded up every cent she had and took a four-day train trip to Washington DC. She couldn't afford a sleeper car, so she slept sitting up in the coach section. When she appeared at the appointed time at the White House gate, she wore a pant-suit, now yellow with age, thick stockings, and a hat older than the Great Depression. She gave her name to the guard, and he looked down his list.

"Ma'am, I'm sorry," he said brusquely, "but your name isn't here and you cannot go in."

"But I was invited!" she said.

"I'm sorry, Ma'am."

A Ford Motor Company executive was also there, and he took Frances Green aside and asked for her story. She recounted her small but faithful donations, the letter, and the long train ride.

"Stay here," he said as he was admitted to the White House. He searched but couldn't find anyone to help her, so he returned and asked, "Can you stay in Washington a day or two?"

"Well, yes," she said. "I had planned to anyway."

"Good. Go back to your hotel and meet me here at nine in the morning on Tuesday."

The man went to Anne Higgins, a presidential aide, and told her Francis's story. Anne went to the president's secretary, and the secretary went to President Reagan. When Reagan heard the story, he said, "When she comes next Tuesday, bring her in here."

On Tuesday the Ford executive met Mrs. Green at the gate and give her a personal tour of the White House. Frances took a wonderful stroll through the historic building, and then they went by the Oval Office at the appointed time, thinking that perhaps she might get a glimpse of the president. Just then the National Security Council came walking out, followed by the Joint Chiefs of Staff. When the executive peeked inside, Reagan gestured for him to come in. Frances Green followed.

When she walked in, the president rose and called out, "Frances! Honey, forgive us, those darn computers fouled up again. If I had known you were coming, I would have come out there to get you myself."

He asked her to sit down, and they talked about California and about her life, giving her the same amount of time he would have given the Queen of England. Though Frances Green never fully understood the lesson Reagan was embodying, the people around Reagan did: Great leaders don't have big heads, but they do have big hearts.

> Great leaders don't have big heads,
> but they do have big hearts.

When people enter my home for the first time, they are often drawn to two official White House invitations personally signed to me and my wife, Teresa, by then President George W. Bush. The story behind how we got these is funny and insightful as to the role kindness plays in the life of the powerful and the not so powerful.

In May 2001 I was serving as the president of the Southern Baptist Convention, and Teresa and I had been invited to the White House for the National Day of Prayer. We were in the East Room for the ceremony, and afterward to our surprise and delight, we were informed that there would be a receiving line so the 150 guests could meet the president. Waiting in line to meet a U.S. president feels unfamiliar. You rack your brain to map out exactly what you'll say, and you try to keep your palms dry so you'll look like you belong there even when you don't.

As we approached the president, a mutual friend who had known him when he was the governor of Texas introduced me to him.

"James, we've met before," President Bush said.

"No sir, I don't believe we have," I said. "I would probably remember if we had met."

"No, James, we've met. I never forget a face," the president said. "It's good to see you again. Welcome to the White House."

He also graciously greeted Teresa, the one of us who looked like she belonged there. She always handles herself with class.

We were escorted to the Yellow Room where refreshments were being served. While there, someone came in holding their invitation, and Teresa and I noticed some writing on it. On closer inspection, we realized it was the president's signature. When I asked the guest how he got the president to sign it, he said, "I just asked for it."

My heart sank as I realized we'd missed our opportunity to have our invitations signed. A line of Secret Service agents flanked the president, and no one could return once they'd met him. But Teresa gave me a familiar look that says, "I'm up to something, and no one can stop me."

"Give me your invitation," she said.

"Why?"

"I'm going to get ours signed as well."

"Teresa, you can't go back out there. You'll get shot!"

She grabbed our invitations and walked back toward the receiving line. Two agents immediately blocked her path and sternly refused her request to approach the president. But I knew the determination in Teresa's face; she was willing to go to federal prison or be deported to Iran for this.

As she pleaded her case to the agents (and I cowered behind a window covering), the president turned and noticed what was going on. He snapped his fingers.

"Let her through," he said.

The agents parted like a Broadway curtain. As she approached the president, he said, "Teresa, how may I help you?"

She told him she didn't want to cause any trouble, but it would be a blessing if he would sign our invitations. He graciously obliged. As he handed the invitations back to her, he said, "Thank you again for being here. Oh…and tell James we really have met before."

Do you think from that point on I was a fan of George W. Bush? Do you think he was now able to impact and influence me? You better believe he was. Regardless of policies I may have disagreed with, from that moment on this president owned my heart.

The fact that these two presidents are Republicans is only a coincidence. Democrats and Republicans, midlevel managers and CEOs, pastors and laypeople, we are all affected by the power of kindness.

The next time you see a helpless lady broken down on the side of the road or hear the familiar melody of "Hail to the Chief," think about the power of kindness. This seemingly small character quality will unlock an inner power that will enable you to change circumstances and shape history. Regardless of who you are or who you *think* you are, try a little kindness with everyone you meet. It will pay off—big time.

> **Principle Five**—*Kindness:* By word or deed, make an opportunity to be kind to someone today.

Chapter Six

Just Be Good

"Goodness is the only investment that never fails."
HENRY DAVID THOREAU

My wife, Teresa, probably doesn't remember it, but I will never forget it. Several years ago she was talking about me to my in-laws (I call them my "in-loves" for they are like my parents). My precious mother-in-law had remarked how she was glad that we had married each other, and Teresa looked at me with that inimitable smile of hers and said, "Momma, I married a really good man." I thought to myself, *And what size diamond do you want to go with that new ring?*

Anyone with a moral compass pointing true north wants to be known as a "good person." I mean, does anyone *really* want to be known as a bad one?

I still laugh when I remember Teresa coming home one time from the grocery store with this horrified look on her face. I asked her what was wrong. She said that she and our oldest son, James (who was about five years old at the time), had been standing at the checkout behind a man who had put a six-pack of beer on the counter. James innocently asked Teresa what it was. My wife smiled and simply said, "Beer." Without warning and loud enough for this man (and half the store) to hear, James pointed to him and said, "Beer? He must be a *really* bad man!"

Like you, I want to be a good man, and I want to live a good life. That statement, however, begs a question: What is goodness and what is the good life?

The French philosopher Jean Jacques Rousseau once said, "Happiness is a good bank account, a good cook, and a good digestion." Many people today would eagerly adopt Rousseau's definition of the good life. Some say that the good life is *physical.* They believe it just doesn't get any better than a hot tub, back rub, and drink at a pub. Others say the good life is *material.* They think that if you've got the mansion, the Mercedes, and the money, *then* you are living the good life.

> Goodness motivates a person to attempt to do what is best for others regardless of the cost.

I beg to differ. The good life is *moral, ethical,* and *spiritual.* Contrary to many opinions, goodness is not feeling good, looking good, or having the goods; it is *being* good and *doing* good. I define goodness this way: *Goodness motivates a person to attempt to do what is best for others regardless of the cost.* It's what some might call character or integrity.

God, for Goodness' Sake

Contrary to much popular thinking, I don't believe that goodness can possibly exist or be known apart from God. If any meaningful standard determines whether something is good, it must be a universal standard; otherwise, goodness is a matter of opinion. David, the great songwriter and king, once wrote, "I said to the LORD, 'You are my Lord; apart from you I have no good thing'" (Psalm 16:2). Indeed, apart from God there can truly be *no* good thing.

After all, Hitler thought the annihilation of the Jewish race was a good thing. Homicide bombers think the killing of innocent humans is a good thing. How can such thinking be countered with a simple, "That is not good"? What is to keep a Hitler or a bomb-toting extremist from saying, "That's just your opinion"?

A universal standard of goodness can be determined only by One who is universally good, and that One can only be God. The very word *good* comes from an Old English word with the same connotation as *God. Good-bye* is an abbreviation of the phrase, "God be with ye." The word *good* literally means "to be like God." The word itself implies that when godliness declines, so does goodness.

Once while in the nation's capital, my wife and I visited the National Archives Building to see the Declaration of Independence. We noticed that the handwritten original was extremely faded and hard to see. Unfortunately, what is happening to this treasured document illustrates what is happening to America itself. The principles, virtues, values, and beliefs that once seemed written on the hearts and minds of this country are fading. At this point, there appears to be little anyone can do to stop the decay.

I recently asked an assistant principal who has been in education for 15 years what she saw as the biggest change that has taken place with schoolchildren. She said, "I know that you would expect me to say demographics with all the influx of immigrants in this area, but the biggest change is society itself. I've been amazed by how the coarseness and loss of goodness in culture as a whole is reflected in the children."

More than 40 years ago, Robert Fitch wrote something that still rings true today:

> Ours is an age where ethics has become obsolete. Morality is now superseded by science, deleted by

philosophy, and dismissed as emotive by psychology. It drowns in compassion, evaporates into aesthetics, and retreats before relativism. The usual moral distinctions between good and bad are usually bathed in a maudlin emotion in which we feel more sympathy for the murderer than the murdered, for the adulterer than for the betrayed, and in which we have actually begun to believe that the real guilty party—the one who somehow caused it all—is the victim and not the perpetrator of the crime.

As a baby boomer, I have witnessed how many things that once were considered either black or white have now been placed in the gray category. Goodness that used to meet a universally held standard is now a matter of personal preference.

> Goodness that used to meet a universally held standard is now a matter of personal preference.

Over the last two decades our country has conducted a national debate on the importance of character and goodness in the private conduct of elected officials, from the mayor of the smallest town to the president of the United States. One of our founding fathers, James Madison, would have been astonished at such a debate. The "first aim" of the Constitution, he said, was to ensure wise and virtuous rulers and to prevent what he called "their degeneracy." Consider what he avowed:

> The aim of every political constitution is, or ought to be, first to obtain for rulers men who possess most wisdom to discern, and most virtue to pursue the common good of the society; and in the next place, to take

the most effectual precautions for keeping them virtuous [read *good*] whilst they continue to hold their public trust.

The second president of the United States, John Adams, concurred. He said, "Public virtue is the only foundation of republics. There must be a positive passion for the public good, the public interest, all her power and glory established in the minds of the people, or there can be no republican government, nor any real liberty."

Adams understood that public virtue depends upon private character. The lack of the latter will always lead to the demise of the former. With a little careful thought, one can see the connection between the private character of a nation's citizens and national peace and prosperity. National prosperity largely depends upon goodness in private character.

If lying, laziness, irresponsibility, dishonesty, and corruption become commonplace, the national economy grinds down. A society that produces white-collar criminals and blue-collar predators has to pay for prison cells. A society with rampant drug abuse will have to pay for drug treatment centers. The demise of families and marriages begs for many more foster homes and lower high-school graduation rates.

> Just as moral goodness leads to tremendous economic and financial benefits, the collapse of morality entails enormous financial and economic costs.

The less goodness exists, the more the government has to intervene—and the higher the cost of governing. Just as moral goodness leads to tremendous economic and financial benefits, the collapse of morality entails enormous financial and economic costs.

Goodness: Doing the Right Thing

Goodness cannot exist in a vacuum, nor does it live in isolation. We measure people's goodness by how they treat others and how they respond in situations where one action is right and the other action wrong. Good people do what is right. John Wesley, the great preacher and the founder of Methodism, said he lived by this one creed:

> Do all the good you can,
> By all the means you can,
> In all the ways you can,
> In all the places you can,
> At all the times you can,
> To all the people you can,
> As long as ever you can.

What a way to live! But *why* is it always important to do what is ethical and moral? Why is goodness the one thing you should go to bed with every night and wake up with every morning? For one thing, even though you see what you are like on the inside, the only *you* others see is on the outside. Proverbs 20:11 says, "Even a child is known by his actions, by whether his conduct is pure and right."

In other words, talk is cheap. No matter how much you claim to be a good person, the only public measuring stick is your actions. You may think that by being good you're not doing a lot of good. But never underestimate the power of even one person to exert tremendous influence by simply doing the right thing at the right place and the right time.

No matter how much you claim to be a good person,
the only public measuring stick is your actions.

Bob Thompson is a case in point. Taskmasters don't come much tougher than Thompson. For 40 years, he pushed his road and highway workers hard six days a week from April to December to finish the job before the first frost. Their loyalty, sweat, and hard work helped make Thompson a rich man.

But recently Thompson returned the favor. He sold his company, Michigan's largest asphalt and paving business, and gave his 550 current and retired employees a $128 million chunk of his gains. Even workers' surviving spouses got checks. Some 90 employees became instant millionaires.

Thompson started Thompson-McCully Company with $3500 that his wife, Ellen, had earned by substitute teaching. The first five years of the business were difficult. Thompson didn't even draw a salary. Why did he later give away so much of his fortune?

"It was the right thing to do," he said. "You realize the people around you have gone through all the pain and suffering with you. I wanted to pay them back."

When the checks were handed out, Thompson stayed away. "I didn't want to be there because it gets too emotional," he admitted.

Goodness: Being the Right Person

Character cannot be manufactured on the outside; it emerges from what a person is on the inside. Being good is not a moonlighting occupation but a full-time job. The person of character is guided by the North Star of goodness that leads him to ask in every situation, "What is the right thing to do?"

> Character cannot be manufactured on the outside;
> it emerges from what a person is on the inside.

One of my all-time heroes is the great former UCLA men's basketball coach John Wooden. He tells of center Bill Walton coming into his office at Pauley Pavilion one day with a serious question. Walton's knees had been causing him increasing pain over several months to the point that just running up and down the court hurt tremendously.

Walton walked into his mentor's office and said, "Coach, I heard that smoking marijuana will reduce the pain in my knees. Is it OK with you if I use it?"

Wooden looked up from his desk and replied, "Bill, I haven't heard that it is a pain reliever, but I have heard that it is illegal."

Classic John Wooden—right and wrong was all that mattered. One of the reasons his players adored him is that they saw in his heart goodness—the unquenchable desire to be the right person and to do the right thing.

As I get older I realize just how important being good and doing good really are. I want my wife to say that I was a good husband. I want my sons to say that I was a good father. I want my church to say that I was a good pastor. I want those special to me to say that I was a good friend. I want those who watched me from afar but never knew me up close to say from my actions that I was a good follower of Christ. I want those under my authority to say that I was a good leader.

One of my favorite presidents was Calvin Coolidge. When Ronald Reagan entered the White House, one of the first things he did was to put Coolidge's picture up on the wall where he could see it every day. Calvin Coolidge probably could not be nominated, much less elected, in this telegenic age. He was a man of few words, even taciturn at times, bred of stern, puritanical New England stock. He would have shunned makeup, the one-liners and sound bites; probably he would have been criticized for an inability to connect with a cutting-edge voting audience.

Why do I admire Coolidge so much? In 1920, when he was mentioned for the presidential nomination, a reporter wrote this of him: "You just have confidence in Coolidge. He may not do what you want him to, he may not do what you think he ought to do, but you know *he's done his best to do right.*"

What a breath of fresh air to hear a reporter say that about a politician. In my mind, that's living the good life. Can you imagine how different our homes, businesses, schools, and government would be if we knew we could count on others and be counted on by others to do our "best to do right"? Cynicism toward government and those who govern festers like a sore on the face of our country. It must be lanced and heal for partisanship to be replaced with goodwill. Goodness is a balm that would hasten that healing.

Finding the Source

Still, where does goodness really begin, and how can we develop goodness and cultivate it in our daily decisions and actions? How can goodness not only survive but thrive in us both individually and corporately?

Some people think goodness is a matter of the *head,* that right thinking leads to right living. Today every politician feels the need to give lip service to the importance of education. They give the impression that improved education is the panacea for practically every problem. Yet education of the head, without an equal emphasis on integrity of the heart, will produce only clever devils.

Robert C. Cabot of Harvard University put it well when he wrote at the beginning of the twentieth century, "If there is not education of men's purpose, if there is no ethical basis at the foundation of education, then the more we know, the smarter villains and livelier crooks we may be. Knowledge is ethically neutral." If education alone could solve our most perplexing problems, then white-collar crime would cease to exist.

Others say goodness is a matter of the *hands*. They say that goodness means treating others well. But doing good does not make one good. Murderers on death row may be good to their mothers, but they are not good people.

Goodness is not found in the head or the hands; it is tucked away in one's *heart*. According to Jesus Christ, who was not only a good man but also the only perfect person who ever lived, "The good man brings good things out of the good stored up in his heart" (Luke 6:45). Goodness is not a matter of what we know or what we do; it is a matter of *what we are*.

Have you ever considered that a musician is judged not by how long he plays but by how well he plays? As you think about the life ahead of you, what really matters is not how long you live but how well you live. Sir Francis Bacon once said, "Of all virtues and dignities of the mind, goodness is the greatest, being the character of the Deity; and, without it, man is a busy, mischievous, wretched thing."

There never is a *right* way to do a *wrong* thing.

My father taught me that there never is a *right* way to do a *wrong* thing. Reuben Gonzales came to the same conclusion. He was in the final match of a professional racquetball tournament, his first shot at a victory on the pro circuit, and he was playing the perennial champion. In the fourth and final game, at match point, Gonzales made a super "kill" shot into the front wall to win it all. The referee called it good. One of the two linesmen affirmed that the shot was in. But Gonzales, after a moment's hesitation, turned around, shook his opponent's hand, and declared that his shot had hit the floor first. As a result, he lost the match.

He walked off the court. Everybody sat in stunned silence. Who could imagine anyone doing this in any sport? A player, with everything officially in his favor, with victory in hand, disqualified himself at match point and lost. When asked why he did it, Gonzales said, "It was the only thing I could do to maintain my integrity." Reuben Gonzales realized one of the greatest lessons we can ever learn in life—we can always win another match, but we can never regain lost integrity.

Every day you will get opportunities to do a good deed, to say a good thing, to show a good heart. These days will turn into weeks, the weeks will turn into months, the months into years, and the years into a life. To strive for anything less than doing good and being good cheats us out of the best.

Someone has observed that people may *have* to work for a bad boss, but they *want* to work for a good boss. As a leader, I want my people to want to work for me. I want to take our organization from "good to great," but we can't be great until we are good.

I have been married over 35 years to a *good* person. Teresa truly is the best person I know. She is sweet, selfless, sensitive—and I dare say sexy to boot! She has been not only a *good* wife, but a *good* mother and a *good* daughter-in-love and a good sister-in-law to my deaf brother. Teresa has modeled goodness in some way practically every day. She is the go-to person for our sons, her niece, her parents, so many friends, and for me because we all know that goodness flows out of her as naturally as water flows from the Mississippi. I often joke that my sons might die for me, but they would kill for their mother!

From caring two days a week for our grandson, to ministering to my 89-year-old mother, to advising her parents on a multitude of issues, to being a combination of Dr. Phil, Dr. Oz, and Martha Stewart to a husband and three sons who in some ways don't want to grow up, she is a walking, talking, living definition of what goodness is all about. I know firsthand the truth found in Scripture that "he who finds a wife finds what is *good*" (Proverbs 18:22). She perfectly illustrates the principle that we all can be good and do good in whatever role we play.

One day we will all stand before the God who is good all the time and undergo a divine audit that will determine just how profitable our lives were to others. In that moment, when the entire universe is silent and we await the only opinion and verdict that really matters, I hope we will hear that word *good* used one last time: "Well done, good and faithful servant." What a joy to know that goodness truly is within our grasp.

Yes, only God is good, but I take great joy in knowing the words, "How great is your goodness, which you have stored up for those who fear you" (Psalm 31:19). God is a wellspring of goodness from which we can daily draw if we allow him to live His good life through us.

Principle Six—*Goodness:* Every day, either take the opportunity or make the opportunity to do a good deed or say a good word—for goodness' sake.

Chapter Seven

Be There

*"One should never trouble about getting a better job, but
one should do one's present job in such a manner as to
qualify for a better job when it comes along."*

CALVIN COOLIDGE

Woody Allen once famously said, "Eighty percent
of success is showing up." Allen is spot-on. After all,
your chance of success is zero percent if you don't
show up!

Allen's advice reminds me of golf. I am an avid, if decid-
edly amateurish, golfer. If you don't show up, you'll never get
better. Furthermore, if you don't connect with the ball, you've
got no chance of advancing the ball. In putting, for example,
I've learned the hard way that the old adage is true, "Never up,
never in." That is, a putt that is even one centimeter short has
no chance of going in the hole. The same thing is true when we
talk about influence and impact. Too many people fall short of
really getting involved with others so that they can earn a place
of influence. They get the ball close to the hole by maintaining
a superficial relationship, but they never get the ball in the hole
by being there when it counts.

You have never heard of him, and probably fewer than a
hundred or so people ever knew his name. Raleigh Matthews

grew up in a little place called Van Zant, Kentucky. That was the official post office designation, but the locals call it Tick Ridge—we are talking w-a-a-a-y out in the sticks. He lived on the same farm for all of his 78 years. He attended Macedonia Baptist Church, a little one-room shack (until they added a state-of-the-art outhouse). It was only a hundred yards from his house and right across the road from the double-wide that served as the pastor's home on the weekends. Macedonia Baptist was the first church I pastored.

Raleigh was already in his early seventies when I first met him. He was soft-spoken and genteel, a walking definition of unassuming humility. On the surface one would have thought he couldn't even influence himself much less others. But it didn't take me long to notice that he had more influence by far than all the other men in the church put together. I was determined to figure out why.

At first, I thought it was all the positions he held. He was chairman of the trustees, chairman of the deacons, chairman of the cemetery committee, the worship leader, and the Sunday school teacher of the only adult class in the church. I just assumed his positions gave him such power and influence. I was wrong.

I had put the leadership cart before the virtuous horse. After a few months as pastor, I noticed a virtue in Raleigh that made me realize why he had been promoted to such stature. This habit gave him incredible influence not only in the church but throughout the entire community as well.

Raleigh was *always there*. It didn't matter whether it was a meaningless meeting or the funeral of an obscure tobacco farmer, he would always show up. When two feet of snow unexpectedly blanketed the ground, Raleigh still showed up for church.

Everyone knew Raleigh Matthews was *faithful*. You could always count on him to show up and give his best. Raleigh had harnessed the power of one.

Serving the 50-member Macedonia Baptist Church in Tick Ridge, Kentucky, I met one of the greatest men and learned one of life's greatest lessons: Faithfulness is critical to influence and impact.

A Vanishing Virtue

Of more than 200 geysers in Yellowstone National Park, one stands above the rest. This geyser is not the largest, and its waters do not reach the greatest height, but it is by far the most popular attraction. This geyser's popularity is due to one thing alone—its *dependability*. People will stand in long lines under a hot sun because according to a precise schedule it shoots a stream of boiling water more than 170 feet into the air. You can practically set a watch by it. That's why they call it Old Faithful. People are attracted to faithfulness.

Without faithfulness, your influence will be limited or wiped out. Without faithfulness, the sum total of your other great talents is diluted. This is the one ability that turns the ordinary into the miraculous and transforms common individuals into dependable achievers. The wise King Solomon asked a great question in Proverbs 20:6: "Many a man claims to have unfailing love, but a faithful man who can find?" People seek out faithful leaders.

> Without faithfulness, the sum total of your other great talents is diluted.

Newlyweds expect their spouses to be faithful to their vows.

Citizens want their politicians to faithfully carry out all their promises, not just the promises they intend to keep. Employers scramble all over the corporate world to find employees who are faithful and dependable.

Unfortunately, faithfulness appears to be another vanishing virtue in this age of quickie divorces, renegotiated contracts, and disgruntled employees.

One employee asked another, "How long have you been working for the company?"

"Ever since they threatened to fire me!" he replied.

Sadly, fear of termination motivates more employees than the joy of being faithful and dependable.

Rush Gets It

The most popular radio talk-show host in America is Rush Limbaugh. He is explosively controversial, but he begins every program with a revealing quote. He starts by saying he has "talent on loan from God." We *all* have talent on loan from God—or, a more familiar way of putting it, God-given talent.

All people on earth have received talents given by their Creator—and each of these talents represents a responsibility to use our God-given abilities faithfully wherever and whenever needed. That is the definition of faithfulness.

Of course, we are not born with equal abilities; some are more gifted than others. *But everyone is born with an equal responsibility to use his or her abilities at full capacity.* That is all any of us can do—and that is exactly what the God who gave us these abilities expects us to do.

> You must give 100 percent of your effort
> 100 percent of the time in all that you do.

We live in a society that tries merely to get by. If you are going to be faithful and dependable, you must give 100 percent of your effort 100 percent of the time in all that you do; 99.9 percent is not good enough.

Insight magazine once published an article called "Strive for Perfection…or Else!" According to the article, if 99.9 percent is good enough, then:

- 103,260 income tax returns will be processed incorrectly this year
- 22,000 checks will be deducted from the wrong bank accounts in the next 60 minutes
- 1314 phone calls will be misrouted every minute
- 12 babies will be given to the wrong parents each day
- 5,517,200 cases of soft drinks produced in the next 12 months will be flatter than a bad tire
- 2 plane landings daily at O'Hare International Airport in Chicago will be unsafe
- 18,322 pieces of mail will be mishandled in the next hour
- 291 pacemaker operations will be performed incorrectly this year
- 880,000 credit cards in circulation will turn out to have incorrect cardholder information on their magnetic strips
- 20,000 incorrect drug prescriptions will be written in the next 12 months
- 107 incorrect medical procedures will be performed by the end of the day

Your best should be good enough in any situation. But anything less than your best will never be good enough because it reflects a failure to be totally faithful and completely dependable.

Be All That You Can Be

For over 20 years, the U.S. Army's recruiting slogan was, "Be all that you can be," suggesting that if you joined the army, they would help you maximize your abilities and reach your fullest potential.

That is God's desire for everyone of us as well. God has invested talents in each of us. Just as people who invest in stocks and bonds expect a return, God expects a return on His investment. In practically every area of your life, you can be faithful to use your God-given abilities for the greatest good of others. Can you think of a better way to leverage your influence and impact on others?

We ought to be faithful, for example, in our *work*. Ecclesiastes 9:10 says, "Whatever your hand finds to do, do it with all your might." Be a faithful employee and do your best at whatever you do. Practically, that means being faithful to

- Come to work on time.
- Stay until the job is finished.
- Do a job that needs to be done, even if it is not in your job description.
- Give an honest day's work for an honest day's wage.
- Take a lunch hour, not a three-hour paid vacation.
- Report expenses accurately and truthfully.
- Uphold the team and the company's reputation.

We also ought to be faithful with our *wealth*. We live in the most prosperous nation in the world. Even the less financially privileged in this country are rich compared to the average person in most other countries. As you think about the money you make and the possessions you have, do you see them as a blessing for you alone to enjoy, or do you see a part of your money as a blessing to share with others?

Do you apply the same standards of faithfulness and dependability to your work life, spiritual life, financial life, and family life that you apply to other areas of your life? For example:

- If your car starts once every three times, would you call it reliable?

- If your newspaper is not delivered every Monday and Thursday, would you consider the delivery service trustworthy?

- If you skip work once or twice a month under false pretenses, would you say you are a loyal employee?

- If your refrigerator stops working for a day every now and then, do you say, "Oh well, it works most of the time"?

- If your water heater provides an icy cold shower every once in a while, would you be satisfied with its dependability?

- If you miss a couple of loan payments every year, does the bank say, "Well, ten out of twelve isn't bad"?

We ought to be faithful to our *word*. I was reared the old-fashioned way, and I thank God for my dad, who is now in heaven, for the upbringing he gave me. One of the things Dad taught me was that I was no better than my word. I still believe that the weakest handshake should be better than the strongest ink on any contract. Remember, your word is not worth giving unless you keep it.

You are not accountable for being *the* best, but you are accountable for being *your* best.

Little Things Are Big Things

How can you develop the virtues of faithfulness and dependability in your life? Dependability begins, grows, and matures by being faithful to the little things.

Too many people today think they are too big for the small things; they would rather get on with what they believe are bigger and more important matters. Longfellow once said, "Most people would succeed in small things if they were not troubled with great ambition."

I have heard people say, "If I had a million dollars, I would do so many things for other people and for God." I doubt it. Most of us would do the same thing with a million dollars that we would do with a hundred dollars—spend it on ourselves.

> Faithfulness can turn even a menial job
> into a vitally important task.

Faithfulness can turn even a menial job into a vitally important task. Just recently I came across this riddle that illustrates dependability and faithfulness. If you can't solve the riddle, see the answer at the end of the chapter.

I represent my country.
I'm always ready for service.
I go wherever I'm sent.

I do what I'm asked to do.
I stick to my task until it's done.
I don't strike back when I'm struck.
I don't give up when I'm licked.
I keep up-to-date.
I find no job too small.
I work well on a team for big jobs.
I'm crowned with a mark of service.

Listen to the Clock

We have now entered a new millennium. But have you ever pondered what a millennium is? A millennium is made up of centuries; centuries are made up of decades; decades are made up of years; years are made up of months; months are made up of weeks; weeks are made up of days; days are made up of hours; hours are made up of minutes; minutes are made up of seconds or moments. Think about it—it's the little things (moments) that make up the big things (millennia).

The other day I asked my beautiful wife if she married me for my looks. "No, I didn't marry you for your looks," she said. "I married you for your brains—it's the little things that count." (Just kidding. My darling wife never puts me down. Besides, I showed how big my brains are by marrying her!)

I'm a big sports fan, and one of my favorite sports is baseball. Every baseball fan likes a "clutch hitter," the player who wins the game with a crucial hit in the last few innings. We tend to admire certain ballplayers who seem to regularly pull the game out of the fire. But amazingly, statistics reveal such players exist only in our minds.

Studies done by pioneer baseball analyst Bill James and researchers for Stats Incorporated have determined that the phenomenon of clutch hitters is a myth. Sportswriters Allen Barra and Alan Schwarz have noted that "what a hitter does in most clutch situations is pretty much what he does all the rest of the time." The statistics even reveal the top hitters in baseball actually average a 13-point *drop* in their batting average when the game is close in the late innings.

> When the game is on the line, it's the
> dependable person you want up to bat.

What occurs on the baseball diamond is no different from what happens in every aspect of life. When things get tough, the person who comes through is generally the same person who *consistently* comes through when things aren't so tough. When the game is on the line, it's the dependable person you want up to bat.

Faithfulness: Return on Your Investment

Aaron Feuerstein owns Malden Mills, a 130-year-old textile company in Lawrence, Massachusetts, founded by Feuerstein's grandfather. On December 11, 1995, Aaron was celebrating his seventieth birthday when he got an urgent call to rush to his company. When he arrived, he saw that three of his factories, covering an area about the size of a track field, had caught fire and burned to the ground.

Where 99 out of 100 people would have fallen into despair, Feuerstein held on to a remote possibility. He noticed the flames had not reached the building that housed the key production unit. As he watched firefighters try to put out the blaze, he turned to his director of engineering and said, "If they can save that building, the mill can stay in business." The executive replied, "You're just dreaming, Aaron."

Malden Mills employed 3400 workers and was the main employer for two neighboring towns. All the workers believed they were going to lose their jobs. All Feuerstein had to do was take the $300 million in insurance money and call it quits, and he would be set for life. But an amazing thing happened.

While the smoke still rose from the charred remains, Feuerstein called his workers together at a school gymnasium. He announced that he was not going to abandon them—that he was going to rebuild the factory. More than that, he was going to keep all 3400 of them on the payroll for one month and give each of them a $275 Christmas bonus.

In the end, every Malden Mills employee received full pay and benefits for *three* months after the fire. All Feuerstein asked in return was their best efforts to rebuild the business.

Just three months later, two of Malden Mills's three divisions were running again at near full capacity. Eighty percent of the firm's employees were back at work. Even though it cost him $1.5 million a week to pay the salaries and hospitalization insurance of his employees, the owner kept his word.

Did the investment pay off? The quality and efficiency of production surpassed its pre-fire standards. One of the rebuilt plants doubled its previous output of fabric. Before the fire, 6 to 7 percent of the manufactured products failed to meet quality requirements; after the fire, that number dropped to 2 percent. When the employees were asked to name the key to the turnaround, they all agreed it was the faithfulness and loyalty of Aaron Feuerstein.

Always Faithful

When the U.S. Marine Corps first formed more than two hundred years ago, officials gave much time to considering an appropriate motto. They finally chose the Latin phrase *semper fidelis,* a phrase today engraved on the mind of every marine. What does it mean? *Always faithful.*

Those are two important words, but the more important of the two is the first. Why? Because it explains how a marine is to be faithful. A marine is not to be faithful only when it's convenient, when he feels like it, or when it will make him happy. *Semper fidelis* means *always* faithful—regardless of the cost. That's why the world's greatest ability is indeed dependability.

For over two and a half years I preached at Macedonia Baptist Church, that little country church I mentioned earlier, and it grew from 40 to 60 people (great growth for a county so far back in the woods they were still negotiating Indian treaties). I preached for the most part to the same people for those 33 months. It would have been tempting to get a canned sermon from a book or steal someone else's message since these people would have never known the difference. I could have had more time to do my seminary class work.

Instead, every Friday night my precious Teresa and I would drive 90 miles to that double-wide after a week of classes for me and work for her. I would get up early on Saturday morning and study all day to prepare my message for the next morning. And I would preach with zeal and enthusiasm as if I were preaching to thousands. (I would even give a Billy Graham-esque invitation, calling hundreds to give their lives to God, even though there were only 40 people there!)

I took my inspiration from an obscure, humble, soft-spoken farmer who never got his name in the paper, was never invited to the White House, was never asked for his autograph or ever appeared on television. Yet his influence and impact lives on in my life today and in the life of a country community in the backwoods of Kentucky for one simple reason: *He was faithful to show up and do his best.*

It is the one thing that God prizes so highly in His creatures. God wants to say the same thing about you that is said about Him: "Great is your faithfulness" (Lamentations 3:23). Whether it is as a boss, an employee, a father or mother, a husband or wife, a friend, or a teammate, become your own marine and be always faithful. People will notice, and they can't help but be touched by your influence and positive impact.

(Oh, yes, the answer to the riddle: I am a postage stamp.)

Principle Seven — *Goodness:* Take every opportunity today to be faithful and dependable, to do your best and be your best.

Chapter Eight

Second Place
Is the First Place to Be

"Talent is God-given, be humble;
Fame is man-given, be thankful;
Conceit is self-given, be careful."

JOHN WOODEN

A fifth-grader came home from school, bubbling with excitement after being voted "Prettiest Girl in the Class." She was even more excited when she came home the next day after the class voted her the "Most Popular Person in the Class." Several days later she won a third contest, but she said nothing about it. Her mother noted her silence.

"What were you voted this time?"

"Most Stuck-Up," she whispered.

At times we all get stuck on ourselves. Keeping the hot air of pride from overinflating our sense of importance is difficult. We are living in the most demanding, individualistic, egocentric culture in our nation's history. At the least insult or slightest remark, we're ready to sue for millions, spout and fume, and gripe and complain as though our children had just been drawn and quartered. We all fight "Muhammad Ali syndrome" thinking we are "the greatest."

Sometimes I think we should change the national motto on our currency from "In God We Trust" to "I Want My Rights."

These days you can't turn right without running into someone's rights. Rights are demanded for children, the elderly, the disabled, workers under 25, workers over 40, alcoholics, the addicted, the homeless, spotted owls, and snail darters.

Rights are considered as American as apple pie. Indeed, this is a country known for citizens' rights. The most familiar part of our Constitution is the Bill of Rights. Rights provide the bedrock of our society, and we should give our lives to defend them. They spell freedom. Our rights protect us from being overrun by an autocratic government. But as Philip K. Howard says in his great book *The Death of Common Sense,*

> Rights have taken on a new role in America. Whenever there is a perceived injustice, new rights are created to help the victims. These rights are different: while the rights-bearers may see them as "protection," they don't protect so much as provide. These rights are intended as a new, and often invisible, form of subsidy. They are provided at everyone else's expense, but the amount of the check is left blank...Rights, however, leave no room for balance, or for looking at it from everybody's point of view as well. Rights, as the legal philosopher Ronald Dworkin has noted, are a trump card. Rights give open-ended power to one group and it comes out of everybody else's hide.[1]

What has the rights movement fostered? A spirit of anything except gentleness, humility, or courtesy. Instead, people are encouraged to "look out for number one" and to get what they want through intimidation, whining, and threatening to sue.

A Kinder, Gentler You

One of the keys in getting along with others is *first getting along with yourself.* You cannot see others properly until you see yourself properly. When George H.W. Bush was inaugurated as president of the United States, he said he wanted America to become a "kinder, gentler nation."

Someone has well said, "Nothing is so strong as gentleness; nothing so gentle as real strength." Just as you catch more flies with honey than with vinegar, so people respond more readily to gentleness than intimidation.

Coach John Wooden told the following story that illustrates a great truth:

> My dad, Joshua Wooden, was a strong man in one sense but a gentle man. While he could lift heavy things men half his age couldn't lift, he would also read poetry to us each night after a day working in the fields raising corn, hay, wheat, tomatoes, and watermelons.
>
> We had a team of mules named Jack and Kate on our farm. Kate would often get stubborn and lie down on me when I was plowing. I couldn't get her up no matter how roughly I treated her. Dad would see my predicament and walk across the field until he got close enough to say, "Kate." Then she would get up and start working again. He never touched her in anger.
>
> It took me a long time to understand that even a stubborn mule responds to gentleness.[2]

I am learning this with my first grandchild. Harper is the apple of my eye. He owns me. Harper loves his "Pop," and Pop loves him. Teresa ("Nana") has marveled at just how close a two-year-old boy has become so attached to me. She remarked recently at how I am gentle and meek around him in a way I never was with my three sons (sorry guys). Harper has a stubborn streak in him that runs in our family, but it seems as if Pop can get him to do things others can't with just a gentle word (and the promise of a Cheeto).

This is something like what Jesus Christ meant when He said in the Sermon on the Mount, "Blessed are the meek, for they will inherit the earth" (Matthew 5:5). The word *meek* refers to a kind, gentle spirit. It implies humility. Jesus said these people will control planet Earth one day, and I think we'll all be grateful when they do. I wish that day would hurry up and get here because the un-meek are making a real mess of things.

But meekness is not weakness. Gentleness is not wimpishness. The words *meekness* or *gentleness* should not conjure up the image of a short, skinny nerd with thick glasses who sings soprano in the church choir. Meekness means *power under control.* An unbroken horse is useless; an overdose of medicine kills rather than cures; wind out of control destroys everything in its path.

> Think of meekness as the security to practice humility.

Think of meekness as the security to practice humility. When Benjamin Franklin was 22 years old, he was living in Philadelphia after escaping an oppressive apprenticeship. He was, as they say, trying to find himself. One question burned in his heart: "What are the greatest priorities of my life?"

In answer Franklin developed 12 "virtues"—the values that would govern his life. They were temperance, silence, order, resolution, frugality, industry, sincerity, justice, moderation, cleanliness, tranquility, and chastity.

Franklin took these 12 virtues to a Quaker friend and asked his opinion. The friend looked at them and said, "Benjamin, you have forgotten the most important one."

Franklin was aghast. "Which one?"

"Humility."

Franklin immediately added this virtue and then organized his life into thirteen weekly cycles, determining that for one week out of thirteen, he would try to focus on one of those virtues.

When he reached 78 years of age, he began reflecting on his life and the qualities he had built his life around. Though he felt pretty good about having achieved most of them, concerning humility he said, "I cannot boast of much success in acquiring the *reality* of this virtue; but I had a good deal with regard to the *appearance* of it."

I can understand why Franklin felt this way. Humility is one of the greatest virtues and character traits known to man—and one of the most elusive. Think about it. We're supposed to show it but *not know it.* If we try to be humble, we have fooled ourselves into thinking we have something to be humble about.

I think of the young, gifted minister who was indeed a good preacher. As his congregation grew, so did his head. After he had delivered his latest masterpiece, a church member shook his hand and said, "You are, without a doubt, one of the greatest preachers of our generation."

It was all the minister could do to squeeze his head into the car as he slid behind the steering wheel. As he and his wife drove back home, he relayed what the church member had said to him. She did not respond.

After futilely fishing for affirmation, he finally looked over at his wife and said, "I wonder just how many 'great preachers' there are in this generation?"

"One fewer than you think, my dear," she said.

Humility is indispensable in developing a gentle, gracious

spirit. Only when we deflate our self-importance and inflate the importance of others can we treat others the way they deserve to be treated.

The Most Important Musical Instrument

Someone once asked Leonard Bernstein, the New York Philharmonic conductor, what the most difficult position in the orchestra was. Without hesitation, the great maestro replied, "Second fiddle." Everyone wants to sit in the first chair, not the second.

The hardest thing most of us will do today is admit our failings and learn to be comfortable with those shortcomings. Think about marriage. For over 35 years I have been married to the most beautiful, wonderful woman I have ever known. We have had our ups and downs, our peaks and valleys, good times and not so good. But I have learned (and am still learning) that when I play "second fiddle," she winds up putting me in the first chair.

> The hardest thing most of us will do today is admit our failings and learn to be comfortable with those shortcomings.

One of the greatest moves I ever made had to do with taking the second chair. When we were going over the plans with the builder of our present home, Teresa had the idea of adding a keeping room to the kitchen. This addition was going to add several thousand dollars to the cost of the house, and I quickly exercised my "head of the home" authority and said no. I said not only would it cost more money, but no one would use it as we already had a den adjoining the kitchen. She said she understood, and I thought smugly that I had won...until I saw the tears in her eyes. I melted, and with a meek and gentle spirit I relented, though I still thought it was a colossal mistake.

The house was built, and can you guess which room is most used by family and friends? The keeping room and the kitchen have become the nerve center for everyone. The den is hardly ever used. My boys still laugh at our near blunder to not include it. Not only was it one smart financial and social decision, my stock soared with a wife who knows that I trust her enough to take the second chair.

Once again I was reminded that often *second place is the first place to be.* Whether it is your spouse, your secretary, or your next-door neighbor, everyone hungers for and responds to those who offer courtesy and gentleness in a spirit of humility.

When Ronald Reagan was governor of California, he gathered up his belongings and left the office early one day. Michael Deaver, one of his assistants, asked him why he was leaving so soon.

"I've just got a few errands to run," Reagan replied.

Deaver said this would happen occasionally, and it always made him curious. On this day he pulled Reagan's driver, Dale, aside and told him he wanted a report the next day on exactly what Reagan had done.

After Reagan left, Deaver looked through the "to read" file that sat on his desktop. On top of the pile was a wrinkled letter from a man stationed in Vietnam. The soldier had written to Governor Reagan, telling him about life in Southeast Asia and how much he missed his wife. He just wanted to tell his wife how much he loved her and how he wanted to be with her. That day was their wedding anniversary, and although the man said that he had already sent a card, he asked the governor if he could put in a phone call to make sure his wife was OK. He wanted the governor to pass on his love, just in case she didn't receive his card.

The next day, Dale told Deaver that Reagan had done more than what the soldier had requested. The governor picked up a dozen red roses and delivered them to the soldier's wife. Dale reported that Reagan approached the woman in an extremely humble way, offering the flowers on behalf of a loving husband stationed in a jungle hell on the other side of the world. Then he spent more than an hour with the woman, drinking coffee and talking about her family.

Maybe that was one of the secrets to the enduring popularity of Ronald Reagan.

The Lesson of the Goats

Do you know how two goats respond when they meet each other on a narrow path above a stream of water? They cannot turn back and they cannot pass each other for they lack even an inch of spare room. Instinctively they know if they butt each other, both will fall into the water and drown. What do those goats do?

> Treat others with the respect they deserve, and they will in turn elevate you higher than you could ever go on your own.

Nature has taught one goat to lie down so that the other can pass over it; as a result, each goat arrives at its destination safe and sound. As Zig Ziglar is fond of saying, "You can have everything you want in life if you will just help enough other people to get what they want." My version of his proverb: "Treat others with the respect they deserve, and they will in turn elevate you higher than you could ever go on your own."

Taking second place to others is powerful in that it actually elevates you above others. Though that seems contradictory, it is true just the same. President Calvin Coolidge once said, "No enterprise can exist for itself alone. It ministers to some great need, it performs some great service, not for itself, but for others; or failing therein it ceases to be profitable and ceases to exist."

What is true for an enterprise is true for an individual. If you will learn the power of second place, you will wind up coming in first every time!

Principle Eight— *Gentleness:* Always make people you deal with feel as if they are more important than you, and treat them that way.

Chapter Nine

Everything Under Control

"He that would govern others, first must govern himself."
PHILIP MASSENGER

A flight instructor was sitting next to his student in their single-engine plane. "Well," he said, "I think it's time to take her in for a landing. Are you ready to go down?" "No problem," the student said. "Let's do it."

As they approached the runway, the instructor looked at his student and noticed his absolute calm. Normally, students coming in for their first landing were nervous, wide-eyed, and sweaty. But this young man looked as cool as the underside of a pillow. The instructor thought, *I cannot believe how calm this young man is. He will make a great pilot.*

Suddenly the plane hit the runway with a thud, bounced 50 feet into the air, hit and bounced again, ran off the runway, and landed upside down in a cornfield. The instructor, upside down and still strapped in his seat, exclaimed, "Son, that was the worst first landing any student of mine has ever made."

"Me?" the student said. "I thought *you* were landing the plane."

> I define self-control as the ability to stay in control when
> circumstances are pressuring you to lose control.

That young pilot may not have been in control of the plane, but he displayed a character trait that all pilots need, for it will mean the difference between life and death. The trait is *self-control*. I define self-control as the ability to stay in control when circumstances are pressuring you to lose control. This young man was able to maintain self-control by believing someone else completely competent was in control.

Out of Control

Today's cultural tree is mostly barren of the fruit of self-control. We live in a society increasingly out of control.[1]

We are *financially* out of control. Americans are the most indebted people on earth, with household debt averaging $71,500—twice that of Great Britain and 89 times that of Switzerland. Our nation's credit card debt alone dwarfs the gross national product of many small countries.

Many Americans are like professional golfer Doug Sanders, who once said, "I'm working as hard as I can to get my life and my cash to run out at the same time. If I can die right after lunch on Tuesday, everything will be *fine*."

We are also *physically* out of control. Did you know that every day in America we eat

- 75 acres of pizza
- 53 million hot dogs
- 167 million eggs
- 3 million gallons of ice cream
- 3000 tons of candy

In addition we spend

- $2 million on exercise equipment
- $3.5 million on tortilla chips
- $10.4 million on potato chips

Every day, Americans drink 524 million servings of Coca-Cola and eat 2.7 million Dunkin Donuts. Still, 101 million adults are on diets. California pathologist Thomas J. Bassler has noticed that in the autopsies he has performed, two out of every three deaths are premature, related to what he calls "loafer's heart," "smoker's lung," and "drinker's liver."

Recent studies from the U.S. Centers for Disease Control say that nearly 60 percent of adults do not exercise regularly. The word *exercise,* like the word *discipline,* really irritates some people. One man said, "Whenever I think about exercising, I just sit down and rest until the feeling goes away." That is precisely why many people die sooner rather than later.

We are *emotionally* out of control. Our highways have become battlegrounds and our schoolyards shooting fields. Road rage is now *the* rage on the highway. Airline rage, grocery store rage, and youth sport rage are reported by the media with unprecedented frequency. If we honk our horns at a stranger, he may use us for target practice. And children are now shooting children, as well as teachers, for almost no reason at all.

James Garbarino, human development professor at Cornell University, reports a major social shift: "There is a general breakdown of social conventions, of manners, of social controls. This gives a validation, a permission, to be aggressive. Kids used to be guided by a social convention that said, 'Keep the lid on.' Today they are guided more in the direction of taking it off."[2]

Garbarino also observes an increasing "culture of vulgarity." Obscenities are now common on cable TV, while violence is promoted in much of today's music. Psychologist Frank Farley of Temple University is concerned about "a loosening of inhibitions promoted on TV talk shows such as Jerry Springer's [in which] it is OK to say whatever is on your mind."

It naturally follows from all this to expect a society that is *morally* out of control. In a 1998 *20/20* interview, Dr. Roy Baumeister of Case Western University said, "If you look at the social and personal problems facing people in the United States—we're talking drug and alcohol abuse, teen pregnancy, unsafe sex, school failure, shopping problems, gambling—over and over, the majority of them have self-control failure as central to them. Studies show that self-control does predict success in life over a very long time."

Without question, we are reaping the bitter fruit of the mentality of the sixties and seventies in which self-control was viewed with disdain by an entire generation. The buzz phrases were, "Let it all hang out," "If it feels good do it," and "Whatever turns you on." The effects are felt not only here but abroad.

"You cannot have happiness without restraint."

Ann Widdecombe, a Shadow Home Secretary for the British House of Commons, once admitted, "Let's face it, we are not a happier society as a result of the liberalization of the seventies. We have record rates of suicides, record rates of teenage pregnancy, record rates of youth crime, record rates of underage sex. We should invite people to recognize that the Great Experiment has failed. *You cannot have happiness without restraint.*"[3]

Our culture reminds me of a man who bumped into an acquaintance in a bar and remarked, "I thought you'd given up drinking. What's the matter—no self-control?"

"Sure, I've got plenty of self-control," he replied. "I'm just too strong to use it."

Whether it's playing a musical instrument, mastering a computer program, or learning a foreign language, any worthwhile endeavor demands self-control. Perhaps that is why Aristotle called self-control "the hardest victory." He also said, "I count him braver who overcomes his desires than him who conquers his enemies."

Self-control is the difference between victory and defeat in the game of life. Those who control self, win; those who don't, lose.

You Must Stay in Control of You

You will never be free of self, but you must be free *from* self if you are going to unleash your ability to influence others. Either you control self or self will control you.

We live in a society saturated with self. Listen to a few recent book titles from religious and secular publishers that have sold like hotcakes:

Love Yourself
The Art of Learning to Love Yourself
Celebrate Yourself
You're Something Special
Self-Esteem: You're Better Than You Think
Learning the Language of Self-Affirmation
Self-Esteem: The New Reformation

Psychiatrists and psychoanalysts have in recent years promoted a movement known as "selfism," which elevates self to the level of god and seeks to avoid anything that would lower someone's self-esteem. Over the last couple of decades, the lexicon of "self" words has been purged of all terms that "selfists" regard as negative. They urge the eradication of words such as *self-criticism, self-denial, self-discipline, self-control, self-mastery, self-effacement, self-reproach,* or *self-sacrifice.* They encourage the use of words such as *self-confidence, self-contentment, self-expression, self-assertion, self-indulgence, self-realization, self-approval, self-actualization,* and even *self-worship.*

Selfism has one commandment: "I am the lord my god; I shall not have strange gods before me."

We see this self-emphasis even in our daily speech. If you are like most Americans, you know 10,000 to 20,000 words (out of a possible 600,000 English words), but you use only 5000 to 10,000 words in everyday conversation.

Twenty-five percent of typical American speech is made up of 10 basic words. A mere 50 words make up 60 percent of our speaking vocabulary. Among the most common words are *you, the,* and *a;* but the most common word is *I.* As Pogo said, "We have met the enemy, and the enemy is us."

> An unhealthy preoccupation with one's self can turn into a selfish desire to gratify the ego at all times and all costs.

I'm not denigrating the need for a healthy self-image. Indeed, that quality is indispensable to the virtue of self-control, for only those who see themselves as they should will be motivated to control themselves as they ought. Yet an unhealthy preoccupation with one's self can turn into a selfish desire to gratify the ego at all times and all costs. And that can be the death knell of meaningful relationships and effective leadership.

Staying Cool: The Hottest Thing Going

If anyone in all of sports ever set a multiplicity of records that may never be broken, it was basketball coach John Wooden. In his 29 years as a college head coach, he had a win-loss record of 664–162—a phenomenal career winning percentage of .804. While at UCLA, he directed an 88-game winning streak and won 10 national championships in 12 years.

Wooden obviously knew something about high-pressure situations, but he was the antithesis of many of today's profanity-spouting, chair-throwing, tie-loosening, fast-pacing, ear-rattling coaches.

He seldom left his seat on the bench, never uttered a profanity (he did utter a "goodness gracious alive" occasionally), never screamed or went on a tirade. Usually he just sat calmly on the bench with his program rolled up in his hand, occasionally giving instructions in a cool, collected manner. Listen to his reasoning: "I tried to teach players that if they lose their temper or get out of control, they will get beat. Modeling was better than words. I liked the rule that we used to have that a coach couldn't leave the bench. I'm sorry they did away with that."[4]

Wooden gained fame for something else—his formula for success in life, known as the "Pyramid of Success." He coined his own definition of success: "Peace of mind which is a direct result of self-satisfaction in knowing you made the effort to do the best of which you are capable." (At the risk of presumption, I offer my version, which ends with "the effort to *be* the best of which you are capable." I don't think Coach Wooden would have disagreed.)

One of Wooden's building blocks in his pyramid is self-control: "Getting to the top, even once, is arduous. Staying there, many say, is even more difficult. My own experience is that both getting there and staying there present unique and formidable challenges. To do either requires great self-control."[5]

People who exhibit self-control are successful in life, a fact that has been clinically proven. In the 1960s, researchers at Stanford University ran the "candy test." They put a large group of four-year-olds in a room and had a teacher tell them, "I am leaving for ten minutes to run an errand. Here are two pieces of candy you may have while I am gone, but if you wait until I return, you can have ten pieces of candy."

After a dozen years, they restudied the same children. They found that those who grabbed the two pieces of candy tended to be more troubled as adolescents and scored an average of 210 points less on SAT tests than the others. The boys who exhibited self-control had fewer run-ins with the law, and their counterparts among the girls were less likely to get pregnant out of wedlock.

> We can't control everything in life,
> but we can and must control the self.

Self-control is a key factor in whether we will be successful. We can't control everything in life, but we can and must control the self. Dr. Baumeister, the expert interviewed on *20/20*, says, "If we're concerned about raising children to be successful and healthy and happy, forget about self-esteem. *Concentrate on self-control.*"

The Power of Self-Control

In countless areas, self-control is vital to maximize your influence and impact. Here are a few areas that are critical.

First, we must control our *time*. Wasted time is wasted life. It takes time to build relationships, learn skills, execute meaningful actions, achieve goals, and fulfill plans. Mismanaged time is the result of a mismanaged life. Time is more than money—it is where maximum impact and influence live.

I cannot tell you the number of times people have said to me, "I'm sorry to bother you; I know your time is so valuable." Listen, *everybody's time is valuable*. No one has any more or less time than you have. The discipline and stewardship of our time is important because our management of time is the management of self.

Believe it or not, time management is not complicated. For years I have made out a list of things I needed to get done, prioritized them in order of importance, and as much as possible, worked my plan, taking one task at a time. Regardless of how you do it, as Nike says, "Just do it!"

The late Peter Drucker was one of the most respected mentors of winners and influencers in America. He said many great things, but none more profound than this: "Nothing else perhaps distinguishes effective executives as much as their tender, loving care of time…Unless he manages himself effectively, no amount of ability, skill, experience, or knowledge will make an executive effective."[6]

> *Self-control* is postponing the impulsive
> pleasure for the important task.

Another mentor and guru, Zig Ziglar, says, "If you will do what you ought to do when you ought to do it, the day will come when you can do what you want to do when you want to do it." Self-control is just that—postponing the impulsive plea-sure for the important task. As this catchy couplet attributed to Benjamin Franklin says:

> Would you live with ease,
>   do what you ought, not what you please.

Control of our *tongues* is also vitally important. Nothing can betray you so quickly as a slip of the tongue. The Bible says in James 3:6, "The tongue is a fire." What awesome power this little member of our body has.

More than a thousand firefighters battled a wildfire for two weeks in the Black Hills of North Dakota. The fire started on August 24, 2000, and was not contained until September 8. In those few days, more than 80,000 acres of prime timberland burned up.

The cause? Apparently a woman stopped on a deserted road, lit a cigarette, and tossed the still-burning match on the ground. Rather than put out the fire, she decided to leave the area. She faces up to five years in prison and $250,000 in fines—but the damage has been done.

In the same way, a rumor, half-truth, sarcastic remark, or angry rejoinder can turn into a lit match capable of burning down acres of office morale, marital harmony, and family unity. Dewey Knight, former assistant county manager of Dade County, Florida, once said, "My best advice came from a friend immediately after I was named to a top county job: 'Son, in this job you will have millions of opportunities to keep your mouth shut. Take advantage of all of them.'" Great advice when you remember you almost never have to apologize for something you don't say.

I remember once saying to my mom when I was really angry, "I hate you." My mom is 89 years old and this happened over

50 years ago, and I can still remember the look on her face. It was as if she had just been shot and left for dead. I was immediately heartsick and apologized, but the damage had been done. To this day I remember the hard lesson of a careless word fired from a mouth out of control.

We must also control our *tempers*. Red hair, Italian ancestors, or even the stupidity of others is no excuse for a short fuse or explosive temper. Do you realize that no one can make you *lose* your temper? Others can only prompt you to *find* it (and make you wish later that you hadn't). Someone has well noted that your temper is so valuable that you should keep it, not lose it.

This day in Kansas City was particularly hot and humid. The eight-hour shift seemed especially long for the veteran bus driver. Suddenly a young female passenger, apparently upset about something, let loose with a string of profane words. The bus driver, looking in his overhead mirror, could sense everyone around her felt embarrassed by the obscenities.

A few blocks later, still mumbling, the angry passenger disembarked. As she stepped down, the bus driver calmly said, "Madam, I believe you're leaving something behind."

"Oh?" she snapped. "And what is that?"

"A very bad impression."

Someone has said, "Winners are those who can stay cool in a hot place, sweet in a sour place, and little in a big place." Ronald Reagan once rightly said, "If no one among us is capable of governing himself, then who among us has the capacity to govern someone else?"

The King in You

One of the strangest, potentially disconcerting, yet most rewarding events of my life occurred as I was concluding my term as president of the Southern Baptist Convention in June 2002. As president I would not only preside over the business sessions of the convention, but I would deliver the presidential address. Normally this is a most gratifying event as you get to cast vision, provide motivation, and generally fire up the crowd to move forward with excitement and enthusiasm to future goals and achievements. But this event was to prove anything but normal.

Prior to this convention, I was pressured by a group called Soul Force to meet and hear their presentation on the Christian morality of homosexuality. I love homosexuals, have several who are friends, and I'm currently in friendly dialogue with a practicing homosexual. But I refused to meet with this group for a number of reasons. They responded with an avowal to disrupt the convention if I refused, which only strengthened my resolve.

As I arrived at the convention center, a number of Soul Force people and others were demonstrating outside. I got out of my car and was shocked to be met by an armed security person who had been assigned to me. The police had been warned of possible demonstrations inside the convention, and I was warned to be prepared at any moment for the unexpected.

All was quiet and orderly in the morning as I presided over the business session. Then later I was introduced to give the presidential address. At first all went well. I was starting to get on a roll when all of a sudden I heard someone yelling at the top of his lungs. I saw a man walking toward the podium screaming invectives and protesting both me and my message. He was quickly grabbed by security and escorted to an exit. Keep in mind I am speaking to over 12,000 people, and they are all watching the protester to see what he is doing and me to see what I'm going to do.

I thought I was in the clear, but then it all broke loose. Protesters started coming in waves, one from this section, one from that section, and for a moment I felt like Custer surrounded by the Indians—as soon as one was grabbed two more popped up. At first I just wanted to scream "Shut up!" I wanted to grab one or two of these intruders on *my* time and *my* stage and in a not so nice way show them why what they were doing was not so nice!

I knew I was at a public crossroads and that my actions at that moment would never be forgotten by me or the thousands who were there. I remember praying, *God, what do I do?* Clearly the answer came back to me—*I am in control of this situation; you just stay in control of you and keep preaching.*

So that is exactly what I did—my voice and determination to continue got stronger with each demonstrator.

Then the moment came. I had just made the statement that people with all their bitterness, anger, and unresolved hostility desperately need God, and we need to offer them God's unconditional love. At that moment a woman was being led by the front of the podium, and she was screaming so hard the veins on her neck looked like mini-Amazon rivers. She looked right at me, and I pointed to her and said, "I am talking about people just like this woman who needs to see from us the love of God we have in our hearts."

Two things happened almost simultaneously: the woman went silent and 12,000 people leapt to their feet and gave a prolonged standing ovation. Rather than responding to the situation with a sharp wit or anger, I composed myself and responded in love. I wish I could describe the feeling I had at that moment, but I knew the self-control I had exercised by God's power had served to maintain control over this entire convention.

> When everyone else is losing control, the
> disciplined person will make the greatest impact
> and have the longest lasting influence.

We all get plenty of opportunities to respond to difficult situations, circumstances, and people with self-control rather than to react according to impulse or selfish instinct. When everyone else is losing control, the disciplined person will make the greatest impact and have the longest lasting influence.

Principle Nine—*Self-Control:* Respond according to principle and what is right. Don't react to the actions of others.

Chapter Ten

Under the Influence

"More often than we e'er suspect,
the lives of others we do affect."
AUTHOR UNKNOWN

The phrase "under the influence" carries negative connotations for many readers. It certainly does for me. One of my close relatives is sitting in a jail cell today because he made a tragic mistake while driving a car "under the influence." Yet, those three words also carry a positive meaning that is far more powerful.

We all are who we are, what we are, and where we are because we were "under the influence" of certain people. I have mentioned many in this book who have influenced me either through the books they wrote or the relationships we had or the advice they gave. I never prepare a sermon that I don't ask, "How would _____ approach this passage?" My parenting approach was greatly influenced through the writings of James Dobson and the loving guidance I was given by my parents. My problem-solving methods to this day go all the way back to my accounting professor, Joe Master, who ingrained in his students the determination to solve even the most difficult accounting problems with rigorous reasoning and indefatigable effort. On and on it goes.

Influence Is Inevitable

The hard truth is *we are all influencers and we are all influenced.* Sociologists tell us that even the shiest introvert will influence 10,000 people over a lifetime. Influence is impossible to escape in either an active or a passive sense. It is like the weather—always there to be reckoned with. Influence is built into the structure of life itself.

Think about our legal system. The very nature of the legal process guarantees that decisions made in one case affect not only the parties directly involved in the case itself, but the rights of others in future cases. This is because of a principle known as *stare decisis,* the concept of precedent. Whenever a decision is rendered in a court case, unless that decision is reversed or modified, other courts follow suit in similar situations. Today every public school in America is desegregated because of one decision—*Brown vs. the Board of Education*—handed down over a half-century ago.

Like a ghost, influence hovers over us wherever we go. We can feel it, but we have to figure out how to remove obstacles between it and us. We have to learn to tap into it. That is why as parents you remain interested and concerned about the people your kids hang out with even after they leave home. We instinctively know that the influence of relationships never diminishes. You want your kids to be a positive influence on others, so you need to protect them from the negative influences that might prevent that.

Someone has called influence the "epicenter of leadership." Truer words have never been spoken. I would add that character is the epicenter of positive influence. Again, everyone has some influence over somebody. It's what you do with it that determines whether it's positive or negative.

Recently I saw *The Blind Side*, one of the finest movies I have seen in years. This touching film tells the story of Michael Oher, a homeless African-American boy from a broken home who is taken in and adopted by Sean and Leigh Anne Touhy, a wealthy white couple who lovingly nurture him into eventually becoming a dean's list student in college and a star football player. This true story illustrates the incredible influence a power-of-one person can have on another.

This doesn't mean that the *result* of one's influence as a leader will always be positive. The past two years have been some of the most painful of my career because I have had to let some people go from our organization for a number of reasons, ranging from economic to performance to just not being a good fit for the job they were trying to do. Yet, if I hadn't made some of these tough decisions, my influence would have greatly suffered when others in the organization knew changes needed to be made.

> Wear your character well and use the power
> that comes with it in a way that positively
> maximizes the impact you have on others.

At the same time, *the greatest influence and impact you have on others comes from who and what you are.* I don't really care what title you have on the outside. Your character will determine if the title fits you. Wear your character well and use the power that comes with it in a way that positively maximizes the impact you have on others.

I have given you nine key character qualities that I am convinced if exercised and seen by others consistently will lift the influence you have on others to its highest possible level. People around the world will line up to follow someone who consistently displays love, joy, peace, patience, kindness, goodness, faithfulness, gentleness, and self-control in their interactions with others and in their responses to even the most difficult of situations.

Yes, I know your question: *How can anyone display all these qualities consistently?* Humanly speaking, you can't. That's the bad news. The good news is, it is not only a possibility but a distinct reality—if you are *under the influence.*

Help Is on the Way

A five-year-old boy fell out of bed, waking the entire household with his cry. After his mother had safely tucked him back under the covers, she asked, "Why did you fall out of bed?"

Between tears and sobs, he said, "Well, I guess I went to sleep too close to where I got in."

Too many people do just that in life—sleepwalk too close to where they began. They fall far short of what God created them to become. The vast majority of people never learn the secret of how to positively and eternally influence and impact people. I didn't randomly pick out the nine qualities we've discussed. These virtues are *fruit*—the fruit of the Holy Spirit. The Bible says that "the fruit of the Spirit is love, joy, peace, patience, kindness, goodness, faithfulness, gentleness, [and] self-control" (Galatians 5:22-23).

> Those who have God's Holy Spirit living
> in them have the supernatural ability to be
> winners who can influence anybody.

These virtues are not naturally manufactured—they are

supernaturally produced. Those who have God's Holy Spirit living in them have the supernatural ability to be winners who can influence anybody. All it takes is being under the Spirit's influence.

The Fruit Comes from the Root

Jesus revealed the secret to getting under the influence in a talk He once gave to His disciples. "I am the true vine, and my Father is the gardener...I am the vine; you are the branches. If a man remains in me and I in him, he will bear much fruit; apart from me you can do nothing" (John 15:1,5). Keep in mind that, horticulturally, the fruit depends on the influence of the vine. To put it another way, a branch bears fruit only if under the influence of the tree.

Jesus said, "I am the true vine." Out of a vine spring forth fragile green buds. Then comes the flower—the bloom ready to mature. And then comes the fruit.

The Creator's will plants the seeds of His image in all of us in order that we might become fruit-bearing branches, reflecting the character of the true vine, His Son, Jesus Christ.

Jesus says, "My Father is the gardener." The only thing that interests the gardener is fruit. He doesn't concern himself about the leaves or the bud, just as God is not impressed with the appearance of the foliage or the flower. He is strictly a fruit inspector. The gardener has one job: to maximize the fruit of the branch.

To ensure that every branch reaches maximum production, God prunes it. Jesus says, "Every branch that does bear fruit he prunes so that it may be even more fruitful" (John 15:2). A gardener prunes in two ways: First, he cuts away fruitless branches that might suck sap that ought to be going to the fruitful branches. If the sap is wasted, the vine bears less fruit. Then he cuts away shoots from the fruitful branches so that all the sap concentrates on enabling that branch to bear fruit.

God's favorite pruning knife is His Word, which Hebrews 4:12 tells us is "sharper than any double-edged sword." God uses this knife to cut and clean the branch. As you read God's Word, God cuts away the bad so it doesn't get in the way of the good, then God cuts out the good so it doesn't get in the way of the best.

> Trials, troubles, and tribulations may simply be pruning shears in the hands of the divine Gardener.

This explains (at least in part) why God allows difficult times to invade our lives. Trials, troubles, and tribulations may simply be pruning shears in the hands of the divine Gardener—tools He uses to cut away dead wood, fruitless branches, and sap-sucking shoots so that we might bear more fruit.

I have had the privilege of spending personal time on two different occasions with the great evangelist Billy Graham. He has embodied the principles found in this book and has perhaps leveraged his life to have more positive influence and impact on others than any person in the twentieth century.

I was awed and humbled to lay hands on this mighty servant of the Lord to pray for him just before he went to preach the gospel to 38,000 people. I knew I was in the presence of a man who literally radiated the qualities outlined in this book. I think of him now because of something he once said: "Mountaintops are for views and inspiration, but fruit is grown in the valleys."

How true. It's easy to love those who love us, but Jesus said to love our enemies. It's easy to be happy when the sun is shining, but difficult when the hail is falling, the thunder is rumbling, and the lightning is crashing. Jesus said, "I have told you this so that my joy may be in you and that your joy may be complete" (John 15:11).

It's one thing to be at peace and calm when life feels peaceful and calm around us; it's another to be at peace when life is caving in on us. But Jesus said, "Peace I leave with you; my peace I give you. I do not give to you as the world gives. Do not let your hearts be troubled and do not be afraid" (John 14:27).

Under His Influence

How does the branch bear fruit? By trying? No. By working? No. By straining? No. The branch bears fruit simply by *abiding*. Jesus said, "Whoever abides in me and I in him, he it is that bears much fruit" (John 15:5 ESV). What does this mean? How does one abide in Jesus? Let me suggest an analogy.

When we put a tea bag in a cup of hot water, something amazing happens to the water. As the tea bag remains or abides in that water, the tea begins to color and flavor the water until that water begins to take on the color and the taste of the tea bag. The longer the bag abides in the water, the stronger the color and taste of the tea.

That is similar to what happens when we abide in Christ and He abides in us. The longer we abide in Christ and the deeper we go with Christ, the more His *influence* will pervade our lives so that we begin to reflect His nature and His character.

The branch does not produce the fruit; it only bears the fruit. The vine produces the fruit. "Abide in me, and I in you. As the branch cannot bear fruit by itself, unless it abides in the vine, neither can you, unless you abide in me" (John 15:4 ESV).

Without the vine, the strongest branch is as helpless as the weakest branch. The most beautiful branch is as useless as the ugliest branch. The best branch is as worthless as the worst branch.

That's why Jesus went on to say, "I am the vine; you are the branches. Whoever abides in me and I in him, he it is that bears much fruit, for apart from me you can do nothing" (v. 5 ESV). The vine produces the sap that enables the branch to produce the fruit. We cannot manufacture these nine winning character traits outside of ourselves—the Spirit of God must supernaturally produce them inside of us. He does that when we abide in Christ and stay under His influence.

But what, exactly, does it mean to abide in Christ? Jesus does not leave us wondering. Jesus tells us that abiding means, first of all, *studying the Word of God.* "If you abide in me, and my words abide in you, ask whatever you wish, and it will be done for you" (John 15:7 ESV). When the children of God look into the Word of God and see the Son of God, they are changed by the Spirit of God into the image of God by the grace of God for the glory of God. That is what abiding is all about.

Abiding also means *doing the work of God.* Jesus said, "Who abides in me and I in him, he it is that bears much fruit" (v. 5 ESV). God is in the fruit-bearing business. That is His work; that is what He desires for us. As we stay under His influence, we will find that our work really becomes sharing His influence with others.

Third, abiding is *obeying the will of God.* Jesus said, "If you keep my commandments, you will abide in my love, just as I have kept my Father's commandments and abide in his love" (John 15:10 ESV). When the branch rests in fellowship with the vine, it reproduces the fruit of the vine.

Getting Under the Influence

A branch without a vine is lifeless. Because it is lifeless, it is fruitless. If a branch is fruitless, it is useless. God wants you connected to Him so that He can give you the supernatural power you need to be the winner He created you to be, that you might influence others to be winners as well.

You make this connection through a personal relationship with His Son, Jesus Christ, who died on a cross and was raised from the dead so that, through faith in Him, we might be grafted as branches onto the heavenly vine and begin to bear the heavenly fruit of His Holy Spirit. That—the right connection—is the secret to being a winner who can influence anybody.

> Ask the Holy Spirit to make you into a tree that
> will bear fruit of blessing on all you meet.

Are you under His influence? Are you connected with God through the only One who can make that connection—His Son, the Lord Jesus Christ? Do you have in you the indwelling Holy Spirit, who wants to bear the divine fruit of these winning qualities in your life?

If so, ask the Holy Spirit to make you into a tree that will bear fruit of blessing on all you meet. If not, I invite you to surrender your life to Jesus Christ, the true vine, who alone can make you a winner whose influence will last for all eternity.

We all remember the little couplet by Henry Wadsworth Longfellow:

> I shot an arrow into the air,
> It fell to earth I knew not where.

But most of us don't know how the entire poem goes.

> I shot an arrow into the air,
> It fell to earth, I knew not where;

> For, so swiftly it flew, the sight
> Could not follow it in its flight.
>
> I breathed a song into the air,
> It fell to earth, I knew not where;
> For who has sight so keen and strong,
> That it can follow the flight of song?
>
> Long, long afterward, in an oak
> I found the arrow, still unbroke;
> And the song, from beginning to end,
> I found again in the heart of a friend.

Longfellow illustrates that even an arrow randomly shot or a song randomly sung will ultimately influence someone or something. Our lives shoot arrows and sing songs daily that influence others, often in ways we may not know or even see. But influencing begins with inviting. We must invite the power of God to fill us and help us manifest the fruit that will transform us into vanguards of influence and impact.

My prayer is that you will be under God's influence so that you might tap into His powerful influence. You *can* make an eternal impact on others. That's what we were all created for. I am grateful for all those people who have so powerfully and eternally impacted me. Forever and always, I will never forget them.

Endnotes

Introduction

1. Cited by Charles R. Swindoll, *Esther: A Woman of Strength and Dignity* (Nashville, TN: Thomas Nelson, 1997), 76-77.

2. Rick Beyer, *The Greatest Stories Never Told* (New York: HarperCollins, 2003), 80.

3. Adapted from Stephen Mansfield, *Never Give In* (Nashville, TN: Cumberland House Publishing, 1996), 29-30.

4. Recently Teresa asked me what I would most like for someone to say about me at my funeral. I thought for a moment and said: "I would love for someone to look at me and say, 'Look! He's moving!'"

5. Paul Aurandt, *Paul Harvey's The Rest of the Story* (New York: Doubleday, 1977), 47.

Chapter One: The Killer App

1. Mark Sanborn, *The Fred Factor* (Colorado Springs, CO: WaterBrook Press, 2002), 108.

2. www.christianhistorytimeline.com/GLIMPSEF/Glimpses/glmps153.shtml

3. David E. Ireland, *Letters to an Unborn Child* (San Francisco: Harper and Row, 1974).

Chapter Two: Joy Ride

1. Victor E. Frankl, *Man's Search for Meaning* (Boston: Beacon Press, 2006), 86.

Chapter Eight: Second Place Is the First Place to Be

1. Philip K. Howard, *The Death of Common Sense* (New York: Random House, 1994).

2. John Wooden, *They Call Me Coach* (New York: McGraw-Hill, 2004).

Chapter Nine: Everything Under Control

1. James Patterson and Peter Kim, *The Second American Revolution* (New York: William Morrow and Company, Inc., 1994), 79.

2. Karen S. Peterson, "Why Everyone Is So Short-Tempered," *USA Today*, 18 July 2000.

3. http://preachingtoday.com/illustrations/search.html?type=keyword&query="Self-control" Italics added.

4. "Interview with Rubel Shelley," *Abilene Reporter-News*, 18 May 2000.

5. John Wooden, "Pyramid of Success," www.coachwooden.com

6. Peter Drucker, *The Effective Executive* (New York: Harper and Row, 1966), viii.

FREE COMPANION SMALL GROUP BIBLE STUDY AVAILABLE ONLINE!

IS YOUR LIFE IMPACTING THOSE AROUND YOU?

"A Valuable Tool..."
JOHN C. MAXWELL

HOW TO IMPACT *and* INFLUENCE OTHERS

9 KEYS TO SUCCESSFUL LEADERSHIP

James Merritt
Founder Impact Men's Conferences

A person's character—who he is—determines the impact he has on others. James Merritt, senior pastor of Cross Pointe Church and host of the television program *Touching Lives*, unlocks nine key character qualities that, if consistently exercised and seen by others, will influence them to reach their full potential.

Readers of this book will be motivated to leave a lasting impact in a number of ways, such as
+ making sure someone sees, hears, or feels love from them each day
+ letting God's joy shine through their life
+ being kind to someone every day
+ being faithful and dependable
+ treating others as more important

No one can do anything about his heritage, but he can do something about his legacy. Beginning today, he can become the kind of person who makes a life-changing difference for others, perhaps even an eternal difference. *How to Impact and Influence Others* shows the way to a life of surpassing influence.

FREE SMALL GROUP STUDY & MORE ONLINE!

Visit the site to buy the book, sign up for Dr. Merritt's daily impact notes via Facebook or Twitter, download a sample chapter and access the free Bible study!

HARVEST HOUSE PUBLISHERS

www.howtoimpactandinfluence.com

Dr. James Merritt is a respected voice on faith and leadership. He is the host of the international television broadcast *Touching Lives* (www.oneplace.com/ministries/touching-lives) and senior pastor of Cross Pointe Church in Duluth, Georgia. Each week, Dr. Merritt's messages can be seen in all 50 states and in 122 countries. He has been featured in several media outlets including *Hannity and Colmes, ABC World News, 60 Minutes,* the *New York Times,* and *Time.*

Dr. Merritt earned a bachelor's degree from Stetson University and a master's and doctor of philosophy degree from the Southern Baptist Theological Seminary. From 2000–2002, Merritt served as the president of the Southern Baptist Convention, the world's largest Protestant denomination, with over 16 million members.

He and his wife, Teresa, are the proud parents of three sons and reside outside of Atlanta, Georgia.

To learn more about other Harvest House books
or to read sample chapters, log on to our website:

www.harvesthousepublishers.com

HARVEST HOUSE PUBLISHERS

EUGENE, OREGON